To –
Hal
with admiration
and good wishes –

# THE CORPORATE CONSCIENCE

# THE CORPORATE CONSCIENCE

by
David F. Linowes

HAWTHORN BOOKS, INC.
*Publishers*/NEW YORK

*To*
*Joanne*
*Richard*
*Susan*
*Jonathan*

# CONTENTS

# PREFACE

The business corporation is caught in the grips of a socio-economic revolution. Twentieth-century man no longer accepts bread alone. Imperceptibly we have moved into a new era, one in which the individual is taking a stand against the onslaught of the institution. This new self-assertion has been evidenced by movements such as Ralph Nader's consumerism; John Gardner's Common Cause; black militant organizations; and all kinds of minority group activists.

An awareness of corporate social responsibility is taking hold. Whether this new awareness is brought about by government pressures, rising social and educational standards of the general public, or the enlightened self-interest of business itself is not important. What is important is that another objective has been added to the profit-making objective of business. The corporation views the world differently now and it relates to others differently; it has taken on a new form under the old name.

The old corporation's structure was directed to one objective only—profits. The new corporation's structure still gives profits the primacy, but now adds bureaucratic limbs to carry on other dimensions, not yet clearly defined. The new corporation is expected to help society fulfill its goals.

This is not to say that material wealth maximization is less important today than it was fifty years ago. Not at all! Profits fund break-throughs in science, higher education, new drug discoveries, government institutions, and massive social programs. Profits are necessary to assure the existence of a business enterprise. When a business organization fails, all persons involved with it lose. Employees lose their jobs, suppliers lose an account, customers lose a product with which they are familiar, and the community loses an economic unit. When a business earns profits and prospers, everyone associated with it benefits.

Over many years of active involvement in my profession, I have felt myself riding the eye of the corporate hurricane. From that vantage point, always I have been impressed with the vigor, dedication, and enthusiasm with which our men of industry have plunged into doing the impossible jobs asked of them. It was the miracle of military arms production that made possible the great victory of World War II. It was the genius of mass production after that holocaust that smoothly turned the swords into plowshares—building homes, automobiles, highways, airplanes, televisions sets.

More so than at any time in the past, business organizations today have evolved into critical components of our democracy. A business and its executives are expected to, and do, participate in the affairs of our society. As informed leaders, business executives are charged with the responsibility of helping make democracy work. Theirs is the obligation, along with material wealth maximization, to view their organization as an essential part of democracy and to involve themselves in the issues of the day.

The business executive stands atop two stilts: to increase material wealth; and to participate as a component of democracy. Both are underpinnings of modern business. To allow either stilt to skid by oversight or by volition must adversely affect the effectiveness of that organization.

One hundred years ago, Ralph Waldo Emerson wrote: "If there is any period one would desire to be born in, is it not the age of revolution, when the old and the new stand side by side, and admit of being compared; when the energies of all men are searched by fear and hope; when the historic glories of the old can be compensated by the rich possibilities of the new era? This time like all times is a very good one—if we but know what to do with it." In this period of socio-economic revolution I am convinced the enlightened business executive knows what to do with it, in spite of the apparent cynicism that sometimes pervades certain sectors of society.

Partly to dispel this cynicism, but primarily for purposes of more effective overall management, giving visibility to a corporation's social concern and action is as important as the fact of having that social concern and taking that action. It is this area of creditable visibility for social actions of corporations that much of this book is about.

In the first several chapters, I write about corporate social responsibility as a phenomenon of our times. Then I proceed to present a suggested means of giving visibility to the social actions and nonactions of a business enterprise. My purpose in designing the Socio-Economic Operating Statement (SEOS) as a form of "social audit" as described in chapters 6 and 7 is essentially to present in concrete form a base from which might be developed a useful, practical, widely adopted third dimension of corporate reporting.

I owe much to many people for the encouragement and assistance they gave me in these efforts and for their comments and criticisms once the concepts were crystallized and exposed. Material contained in several chapters in this book benefited greatly from constructive comments received when the early proposals were presented in address and article form.

Among those to whom I am especially indebted for their critiques and commentaries are: C. L. Scarlott of Exxon Corporation; Walter A. Albers, Jr., of General Motors Corporation; Bernard L. Butcher of Bank of America; John C. Burton of the Securities and Exchange Commission; Raymond A. Bauer of Harvard Business School; Ralph F. Lewis of *Harvard Business Review*; Abraham J. Briloff of Baruch

College; Daniel H. Gray of Arthur D. Little, Inc.; Sybil C. Mobley of Florida Agricultural Mechanical University; and my partner John D. Lesure of Laventhol Krekstein Horwath & Horwath.

Without the research and manuscript preparation assistance of Raymond Dreyfack, this work would have dragged on for years. He always kept the pace stimulated, especially when the pressures of my other obligations often forced me to want to put this aside. My secretaries, Mrs. Judi Rieger and Mrs. Susan Weintraub, performed the painstaking typings and proofreadings of each of several drafts with dedicated loyalty and effectiveness. I am grateful to each of them.

I find the great thing in this world is not so much where we stand as in what direction we are moving.
—Oliver Wendell Holmes

# THE
# CORPORATE
# CONSCIENCE

# 1
# BY CHOICE
# OR BY LAW

I can remember when functional lines between private and social enterprises were readily drawn. "Public sector" meant one thing, "private sector" another.

Today the two terms overlap. Corporate actions increasingly affect social conditions. Private rights of way cross public thoroughfares. Private and public activities interact in key segments of the economy.

Take the large corporation. Its mere presence in a community shapes life styles and standards. Big industry in particular: auto, construction, petroleum. It exerts far-reaching impacts on the health, economy, and aesthetics of urban and suburban areas.

In broader context, consider the emissions and wastes of production. Uncontrolled, in time these could deaden the planet. Or the proliferation of products for which need is questionable, desire artificially stimulated. Unchecked, what proportion of earth's dwindling energy resources might be needed to produce this vast accumulation and dispose of it after consumption?

The need seems self-evident. Somehow or other controls must be applied to corporate activities. If our system is to survive, companies can no longer make major decisions without taking into account the social consequences of their action. Despite the contentions of laissez faire–advocates, well intentioned or not, the evidence mounts that a Friedmanic preoccupation with profits alone is myopic and destructive, not only to society but to business as well.

The reality is blunt and conclusive. Society is dependent on business. Business is a dependent *of* society. The corporation cannot realistically or rationally divorce itself from society's cotenants. Socially constructive corporate action will in the long run benefit all of society. Irresponsible action—or inaction—will boomerang to harm business as well as the nonbusiness sector.

## Social Goals and Profit Roadblocks

If it's all so obvious, where's the problem?

The solution seems simple enough. Let's apply it to Whambang, Inc., a typical manufacturing company. Step one, call a meeting of the board and explain the need to directors.

"You see, it's like this, gentlemen. What we'll have to do is build into our master plan some positive social programs designed to upgrade quality of life along with quality of earnings."

"Why us, and how much money are we talking about?"

"I'd say annually about one or one and a half percent of the company's net worth."

"One and a half percent! That's a heavy load for our shareholders to carry. Why should we go along with that kind of commitment?"

If corporations went along with it, our social problems might be well on their way toward solution.

But why should they go along?

For one thing, they have corporate goals to contend with, plus the quotas and milestones they generate. These necessarily zero in on the hard profit lure that triggers investor and executive interest. Managerial pressures all converge on this aim. Career aspirations are linked to it.

It would be hard to find a manager who isn't gung ho for social reform—elimination of poverty, reduction of crime, clean water and air. But the machinery of involvement needed to rank social goals alongside income goals has yet to be worked into the system. Until this occurs, the temptation to rationalize nonparticipation will remain too strong to resist.

Repeatedly, I hear it.

"We're only one company. We can't cure social ills alone. If we invest in social programs and our competitors don't follow suit, it will place us at a disadvantage in the marketplace."

This last would be hard to refute.

I know of a New England electronics producer who recently sent an announcement to customers. What it boiled down to was: We don't like to do it, but we have no choice. Due to rising labor and materials costs, we are raising the price of several items in our line by approximately 5 percent.

The company lost several customers as a result of this action, profits sagged. What hurt was that its leading competitor was able to hold the price line.

It is considered significant by some in the industry that Company One, the price hiker, had during the previous year voluntarily made a substantial investment in pollution control equipment. Company Two, as much a pollutor as Company One, didn't invest a penny.

Company One's president is understandably bitter. "That's our reward for good citizenship," he complained to me. "If we hadn't installed that equipment, I think we might have held off on those price boosts."

His complaint is worth noting.

If Chrysler puts large sums into social-action programs independently of Ford and GM, it could wind up in serious trouble. If United Airlines launched an ambitious hiring and training program for unschooled minority workers while key competitors stood by uncommitted, it might yield an ill-afforded edge. Realistically viewed, corporate chiefs cannot be expected to push for sizable social programs that are likely to make financial statements look bad and management worse.

Companies today are in the micro–macro bind. Short-term corporate aims—the profit and loss (P&L) syndrome —serve insidiously to undermine long-term corporate gains.

Take a program to upgrade unskilled workers, for example. Over the long pull it will give them pride and self-sufficiency, reduce welfare costs and crime. Who has more at stake than business in the fulfillment of these social goals? Such programs are not only humane but pragmatic. But it's not pragmatic for Company A to spend large sums on social improvement while its chief competitor, Company B, sits back and coasts. In the long run Company B would benefit from the investment at no cost to itself. It would be like gratuitously conducting a research program for a competitor, just cause one might say to get a chief executive tarred and feathered.

So what does Company A do? Ignoring its twinges of conscience, it cautiously monitors Company B. Equally wary, Company B does the same. Each waits for the other to move. But society, beset by deepening crises in its cities, prisons, schools, hospitals, and environment, is hardly in a position to wait. The longer the wait, the greater the threat to all sectors involved, the private sector included.

The solution? It's as simple to state as it is difficult and complex to get rolling.

What society needs, in my opinion, is a system of measurement and reporting that will permit the intelligent reviewer to compare points of likeness and points of difference in the social actions of individual companies within each industry. Comparability does not imply absolute uniformity of accounting, nor does it permit unrestrained flexibility. The system would supplement traditional profit goals with social needs linked to corporate functions.

Today's business and social planners disagree sharply

over the parameters of social responsibility. Executives can't pinpoint what the term encompasses, how far it should go. But sociologists and business executives working together have enough information today to start to set nationwide guidelines and standards for the business community.

The job won't be easy. But we have much of the data on hand. We have the tools and techniques that we'll need. Innumerable social programs can already be quantified. Some headway has been made toward the measurement and reporting of the complex actions that are tougher to quantify. Trial and error will be needed and in some cases compromise. But isn't this always the case when new concepts emerge?

The conflict strikes a note that's been heard often before. We bucked flaming controversy in the past when economic measures and indicators were first tried. These have never been refined to the satisfaction of all. Nor are they ever likely to be. But fumblingly or not, they were developed and implemented. Today they're applied, if not flawlessly, with a fair degree of effectiveness. They serve a useful role in society.

The current rhetoric over social measurement and reporting is reminiscent of those early days when various securities and accounting guidelines were initiated. Hot hassles prevailed. Today's arguments advocating deferred social reporting until definitions are clearer, better consensus achieved, more exhaustive study made, are eloquent echoes of those bygone days.

Who's to define how much research is enough? Will social scientists ever agree on this? Will true consensus regarding rules ever be reached? Will social crises in our cities and institutions remain in suspension until "action now" finally happens?

History should have taught us by now that guidelines don't spring up overnight. Like fine sculpture, they emerge slowly and gradually. Accounting principles took decades to develop. But they weren't formally compiled into book form until after World War II, and they are still a long way from fully refined. With regard to still virgin social reporting, it's a matter of getting to work on the unformed wood, stone, or clay. It's a matter of molding and standing back to assess, chipping and forming, adjusting and correcting until the right shapes develop. Since the beginning of civilization this process has taken place in various segments of society. No reason I can conjure, especially in view of the urgency, would make the socio-economic sector an exception.

We've delayed long enough. We can't afford to compound past mistakes with more squabbling, ax-grinding, and philosophical debate. It's time for all concerned parties to join the same team.

## The "Or Else" Factor

I've talked with scores of leaders, business, political, social. Most of them—even those who recommend delay—agree social measurement and reporting are on the way. In the foreseeable future such reporting will be as familiar to businessmen as the cash flow statement is today. It is simply a matter of when.

It is also a matter of "who." Who will lay down the guidelines and rules? Who will monitor the actions and set reporting requirements for companies to follow? These questions are of vital concern to every corporate leader.

The alternatives are sobering. Social measurement will develop in one of two ways: by multidisciplinary task forces—businessmen, government officials, social scientists, and other professionals getting together to iron out differences and set up guidelines—or, failing such rapport, the rules of the game will be prescribed by big government.

We've seen it happen often enough to convince us.

A dock strike impends with business paralysis threatened. Big government steps in to mandate work resumption.

Rail unrest brews. Truckers threaten to shut down.

Phone talks strike an impasse and workers walk out. Big government intercedes, directing labor and management to get back on the job for a "cooling off" period.

Meat prices skyrocket beyond reasonable levels. Steel proposes new hikes that will send inflation soaring higher. Big government turns thumbs down and the price boosts are killed.

Such unilateral control is essential at rare times when emergency strikes. But under a free system of government and enterprise, a key operational word is "voluntary." Of one thing I'm convinced: The less voluntary social action U.S. companies take, the more it will be imposed by big government. This course seems inevitable. The longer corporate social action is deferred, the more certain we can be that emergencies will erupt.

When people start choking in the streets, big government will have no choice but to shut down polluters. When riots explode because blacks can't get jobs, big government will mandate hiring and training programs. When waste grows unmanageable to the point where either people or products must go, big government will tell companies what they should produce and how much.

Is that the way we want it? Most businessmen and lawmakers agree—some quite vehemently—that big government already has imposed too many rules and controls.

A *New York Times* writer states:

> It is . . . obvious that the more detailed and rigorous Government regulations are, the more extensive and oppressive will be the enforcement apparatus that is required. Regulations that are all encompassing and detailed in prescribing required conduct can be enforced only by a totalitarian police state.
>
> To avoid the necessity of detailed prescriptive regulations, business must voluntarily assume the burden of social responsibility and responsiveness to changing contemporary social needs. Business cannot generally

wait for legal compulsion to do that which the public expects and demands of it, and it cannot properly limit its performance to the bare minimum tolerated or required by law. To do this is to assert implicitly that Government control is necessary and that freedom of action will be used only for self-seeking activities. This is a flouting of the ethical responsibility of business.

Business must do what is right by contemporary standards without being compelled to such performance by law.[1]

The message comes hammering through.

Take Slumville, New York. A social job is there to be done. The area is exploding—and explosive—with seething minority youths aged fifteen to twenty with time on their hands and trouble on their minds. Their minds: resources that have never been properly used. But the community is run down. A scarcity of money and talent exists.

Four major corporations dominate the area, providing most of the employment. If each waits warily for the other to act, the situation will drag on and get worse. Drug dependence will multiply. Mugging and vandalism will rocket. Fear, bitterness, and distrust will deepen. At some point all hell will break loose.

But if managers from each of the four companies sit down with social and government leaders to thrash out a solution, the prospects are good for success. Hiring, training, recreational programs will emerge. We can expect no utopian solutions, but progress will result.

We saw it happen in Kansas City, Missouri, where a dedicated multidisciplinary team of businessmen, politicians, and social planners converted a deteriorating health care system into an effective modern service center. We saw it in Fresno, San Jose, Pasadena, and Anaheim, California, and in Tacoma, Washington, where business and city government professionals jointly apply their diverse talents to social problems at hand. We saw it in New York City's school system, where in an Economic Development Council–venture business managers on loan help educators and social planners to tackle and solve high school dropout, violence, and low achievement problems, with dramatic results tabbed to date. We saw it and continue to see it in scores of communities and institutions across the United States where a diversity of professionals combine resources and skills to meet common goals of social achievement.

Multidisciplined cooperation and coordination will make the throes of reform less taxing, the process more efficient. Businessmen are long accustomed to measurement, evaluation, monitoring, and reporting techniques. No segment of society is more qualified to set up the standards and guidelines required.

Technology transfers—adopting proven techniques and technology to new applications—is a science business developed.

As one chief executive put it to me recently, "Creating a corporate social responsibility system with business itself as a major participant is the only sane way I can see to proceed."

The alternative is equally clear—still more government controls, restrictions, and mandates. An alternative to ponder.

### The Forces of Change

A converging mix of pressures in our society is at work and accelerating to make "action now" more urgent than ever.

As I have indicated, the existing system is patently unfair to the sincerely conscionable corporate activist. The machinery to assess and report the social consequences of corporate actions and omissions has yet to emerge. Until that occurs, the P&L syndrome must inevitably prevail.

Sophisticated financial analysts can't ignore the realities.

Managements that fail to replace marginally productive equipment and defer training or research programs have higher short-term earnings than those that invest in the future. In time, the neglect takes it toll. Talented comers resign. Operating effectiveness sags. Product development falters while market share diminishes. But for the short run, at least, the penny-pinching scrounger looks good.

The way things stand today, it works the same way for the social condition.

A nationally known mining and manufacturing company annually ravages and defaces untold acreage in a dozen U.S. states, converting virgin stretches of land into unsightly eyesores via strip mining procedures. In no way is this social destruction reflected on the corporation's financial statements.

The same company contributes thousands each year to community renewal and neighborhood improvement programs. This is not reflected, either.

The handful of companies whose social improvements truly exceed their detriments are beginning to understand the price they must pay for good citizenship on the P&L statement.

A prominent banker complained to me recently, "We set up hiring and training programs for hard-core unemployables; we loan high-paid executives to government agencies; we invest money and time to help ghetto entrepreneurs. So far as the statements are concerned, they're all operating costs which reflect against management."

As things stand today, the worst corporate abusers are paraded in most favorable review before shareholders and potential new investors.

The chief executive of a multinational manufacturing company spelled out in frank terms a growing top management dilemma. "On the one hand, the pressures are building to step up social action and investment. On the other hand, stockholders are clamoring no less vociferously than in the past for hiked profit performance. How can you rationally reconcile social investment without being able to show its scope and importance objectively? We need a measurement and reporting vehicle to offset conventional statements in the eyes of stockholders, employees, and critics."

Lacking objective, standardized reporting, managers are understandably reluctant to discuss social programs and plans. Others are fearful of exposing new cans of worms to public scrutiny. Still others are fearful of alerting regulatory agencies and consumer activists to their neglect. Thus only rarely is social reporting comprehensive and meaningful.

I know of one American corporation under attack from various agencies and citizen groups. It is without question one of the nation's most flagrant social offenders. But it is not unmindful of its public image. For every thousand dollars worth of damage it does a dollar's worth of good.

In this company's annual report its nobility is given beautiful public relations treatment. Its institutional advertising is a masterpiece of self-adulation. Its company publication regularly and persuasively hammers home a message of good citizenship to employees.

Blatant or not, this follows a generally classic pattern. PR-generated image messages of this kind range from subtle self-glorification to outrageously transparent puffery—but transparent only to the thoughtful and intelligent observer.

A study by the nonprofit Council on Economic Priorities makes the situation clear: "Those companies which tend to contribute most to pollution also tend to toot their horns most blaringly about the contributions they make to pollution control."

An oil company, for example, periodically reports its investment in antipollution equipment and research in glowing terms. The dollar figures are impressive to the uninformed reader. But close examination reveals that the investment cited is a mere fraction of what it should be in light of the company's earnings and size.

It seems clear that corporate social reporting will continue to have low credibility and serve as little more than window dressing until measures and standards are established.

## *Dynamite Charges and Verbal Blasts*

Two decades ago "corporate conscience" referred mainly to working conditions, fair wages, fringe benefits; secondarily to such aesthetics as landscaping.

We've come a long way since then. During the Vietnam debacle a devastating transition took place in America. We became a nation in crisis. Black power, woman power, consumer power, senior citizen power, student power came into being. Deprived citizen segments grew increasingly wrathful and vocal as new leaders emerged and new action strategies developed. During the transition the concept of social responsibility took on new meaning and scope.

Today the term encompasses virtually all aspects and issues relating to quality of life and the social condition. Hopefully, the corporate conscience in this last quarter of the century will be conscientiously applied. If so, it will be concerned with the ecology, consumer interests, the nature and rewards of work, minority aspirations, community development, the social implications of products and practices, a whole lot more.

None of this happened by accident. A tidal wave of citizen action militated to produce it. Perhaps most notable was the forming of innumerable dissident groups, structured into onslaught vehicles of unrelenting social change. A case in point is the environment. Whole directories now exist listing action and research groups concerned solely with protecting and preserving the ecology. Spotted nationwide we find Friends of the Earth, Citizens for Clean Air, Campaign Against Pollution, The Wilderness Society, The Sierra Club, Citizens League Against the Sonic Boom,

Defenders of Wildlife, Ecological Society of America, and many more, with the roster growing monthly.

Other groups home in on other specialized areas of social improvement. The National Security Research Project, Institute for Southern Studies, Clergy and Laymen Concerned, and others concentrate on activities of the military-industrial complex and monitor companies engaged in military work. Other groups press for change in such areas as foreign investment and activity, labor and minority practices, public health and safety, consumer protection, and more. Organizations like Committee for Responsible Corporate Action, Council for Corporate Review, Council on Economic Priorities, and Ralph Nader's Center for the Study of Responsive Law, to cite a few, target specifically on corporate social responsibility.

Other groups are out-and-out revolutionary. Altogether they possess a formidable and fast-growing arsenal of weapons to combat the socially irresponsible corporation. Tactics range from boycotts and annual meeting disruptions to bombings and mayhem by the lunatic fringe.

At a recent meeting in New York, Walter B. Wriston, distinguished chairman of First National City Corporation, rose to address his large audience. He appeared nervous and anxious as he attempted to defend his company's minority hiring practices and Citibank investments in South Africa. A visitor from the sixties would have been shocked; a decade ago such an action was unheard of. Others on the corporate griddle over the South Africa issue include such giants as Ford, Exxon, Caterpillar Tractor, Gulf, ITT, 3M, and a host of comiserants.

Corporate targets proliferate, and the ammo's not buckshot. Take the Pittston Company, for one. New York's Field Foundation is an important institutional investor holding Pittston shares. At last report it had submitted three proposals to the company requesting: (1) that it make periodic reports on how West Virginia flood victims created by a company dam collapse are being compensated; (2) that a public policy committee be formed to work on mine safety and ecology measures; (3) that the company report the proceedings of each annual meeting to shareholders.


## Religion at Bat

Religious groups are growing increasingly aggressive and vocal on the responsibility front. The National Council of Churches, for one, has set up a Corporate Information Center to coordinate activities and provide social information for churchmen and public alike.

States Director Frank White:

> The Church is important in the battle for corporate responsibility for two reasons. First, of all the potential institutional participants in the battle, such as foundations and universities, the Church sees itself in society as the locus of moral and ethical initiative. On this basis the Church is vulnerable to raising the issue. Secondly, the Church has clout. Church wealth has recently been estimated at over $160 billion, more than the combined wealth of AT&T plus the five leading oil companies. It is second only to the Federal Government in monies received and distributed yearly—over $22 billion.[2]

A key Center function is to develop investment policy procedures and other strategy options. These include counselling privately or by petition with management about corporate policies that prompt investor concern. It organizes public hearings on the social costs and consequences of corporate actions. It formulates stockholder proposals to change corporate policy, collects proxy votes on annual meeting proposals, makes the Church position known. The Center also works with outside groups to influence corporate decisions. It institutes stockholder class-action suits, a thorn which has taken on swordlike proportions in recent years. It refuses—and publicizes its refusal—to invest in companies whose ratings fail to meet established social responsibility standards.

Religion against the corporation moves a giant step beyond theory. An example is the recent Clergy & Laity Concerned (CALC) action against Honeywell. CALC is a nondenominational group with fifty-three thousand members in fifty U.S. chapters. Honeywell's 1973 proxy statement included a CALC proposal asking the company to stop production of "antipersonnel weapons." CALC prefaced this with a year-long campaign. It urged consumer boycotts of Honeywell products and student demonstrations against Honeywell recruiters. It also asked city governments in Ann Arbor, Michigan, Palo Alto, California, and Boston not to buy Honeywell products. At the company's April 1973 annual meeting in Minneapolis, CALC members turned out in grand and vociferous numbers.

## Profiles and Buildings

It's no secret that publicly held companies long have been touchy about their marketplace profiles. The new crusaders are gleefully aware of the long-lasting wound that can be inflicted on the company clapped in the public stockade as polluter or discriminator. The potential damage to its profile was a key factor in American Standard Corporation's 1970 decision to pay $15 million in settlement of four antitrust class-action suits.

Class actions have proliferated like cucumbers in the United States in recent years. A 1973 *Fortune* survey reveals that two-thirds of companies responding admit they are presently involved in or threatened by class-action suits.

Now, the report notes,

> a move is afoot in Congress to permit individuals to aggregate claims. That would open up the possibility of broad attacks by consumers, and corporations eyeing the proposed legislation are naturally somewhat upset by it. Says a lawyer who is helping to frame the legislation: "These people are really scared. The ironic thing is that most consumers are still completely unaware of the possibilities for class action. One can only wonder what the situation will be when all the groups that can stand to benefit have marshalled their attack."[3]

"Class action" has a meaning of its own to the radical fringe. Recent years have seen a marked increase of explosive and incendiary bombings directed against banks, public utilities, railroads, and other industrial facilities; not to mention kidnapping and assassination attempts on the lives of business leaders in a misguided effort to influence corporate policy.

On top of it all, corporations are feeling the political squeeze.

One politician, en route to a mountaintop meeting of a conservationist group, remarked wryly to an aide as their car climbed toward the summit: "There's votes in them thar hills."

Tongue in cheek or not, politicians traditionally move in response to constituent urgings. On their own or through activist groups, more and more people these days are making their views known to representatives in office. Political comers in particular are alert for new ways to capture the public imagination and cash in on citizen indignation, ready and willing to play touch football with touchy issues. Incumbents with their hierarchies at stake are quick to respond.

In short, it is no coincidence that a rash of government-formed councils and agencies now deal with hot issues ranging from consumer rights and the ecology to equal treatment of women, senior citizens, and deprived minorities.

Nor is the working man neglected. Big labor has a crusade of its own to monitor hiring, work conditions, and labor practices.

### The Stirrings Within

Corporate leaders have not slept blissfully through all this transition. Many are aroused and disquieted.

A friend who serves as executive vice president for a major eastern corporation admitted to me frankly: "The external pressures may seem overwhelming at times. But that's only half the problem. The pressures inside can be worse."

Internal stirrings stem from a number of sources. I consider it highly significant that out of the turmoil and tumult of the sixties and seventies has emerged a new breed of manager. He is typified by retired GM Public Relations Vice President Paul Garett, who notes that "the chemistry between business-for-profit and the society in which it functions should be one of the first priorities of top management."

Many executives take this to heart. Like everyone else, the conscionable businessman is caught up by society's sickness and pressing need for health maintenance. Many social activists are corporation bred. I am personally acquainted with several chief executives, for example, who are avid sportsmen and dedicated conservationists. I know others as much sickened by prejudice against women, blacks, and the elderly as the most outspoken campus critics. Still others lash out against irresponsible production policies with as much vehemence—and more reasoned judgment and objectivity.

Most managers are endowed with better than average intelligence and sensitivity. They recognize that without social restructuring, corporate profits over the long haul will be an empty objective. And like other citizens they have children and grandchildren.

On top of it all we have the long-range profit plan. I see a new awareness among far-sighted business leaders that despite the much-publicized high costs of social renewal there's money to be saved and made when the turnaround begins. I'll explore the profit potentials of social improvement more deeply in another chapter. For now it's enough to say that when a society is sick, the costs are borne largely by business. These costs run the gamut from the marketplace impact of the fractured company profile to heavy taxation and out-of-pocket expenditures for security safeguards, maintenance, and repairs.

Social improvement already has developed into a new burgeoning industry. The hottest issue of the day, its potential is exciting to imaginative entrepreneurs. The company that can generate new ideas, technology, service, and equipment beneficial to society will find a growing market for its output.

This explains in part why, as Conference Board President Alexander B. Trowbridge points out we're witnessing important policy, organization, and operations changes in progressive corporations. Typical innovations include:

• Public affairs departments set up, new vice presidencies created.

• Revised hiring, training, loan policies.

• Pollution control procedures to pretest and monitor the ecological effects of new products.

• Increased dialogue with youth and minority groups.

• Encouraged employee participation in community affairs.

• Framing corporate social performance as well as profit objectives. (Difficult to achieve on a fair matching basis without nationally uniform social measurement and reporting.)

• Revamped corporate contribution programs.

The Conference Board mailed social responsibility questionnaires to senior U.S. executives. In response, searching new questions were posed.

1. What are the guidelines for defining and measuring the social responsibility of business?

2. What is the division of responsibility between business and government in areas not previously considered to involve business directly? For example, environmental pollution, urban blight, drug abuse?

3. How does one factor social issue costs into the corporate profit and loss sheet?

4. Should institutions and foundations vote shares of stock on the basis of social and ethical issues, and what are the nonfinancial criteria?

5. How can business help set national goals and priorities to which the entire nation can subscribe, as a framework in which business management could then set its goals?

6. How can business communicate more effectively with the public to ensure better understanding of the very complex problems imposed by social change, and also of the positive role of business in social as well as economic progress?

7. What can business do about obsolete government regulations in areas of antitrust laws, or labor relations and foreign trade and investment, which hinder social solutions?

8. What role are universities assuming in research and evaluation of current programs and in the field of social issues?

9. What are the social implications of the current antipathy to science and technology?

10. What amount of time and talent of senior operating executives should be devoted to adjustment of the corporation to social change vis-à-vis normal operation responsibilities?[4]

## New "Rules of the Game"

New rules for measuring and monitoring corporate social responsibility are urgently needed and inevitably on the way. No thinking man would dispute this. As the Corporate

Information Center notes: *"Life and death are more important than profit and loss!"*

The crucial question is not: "Will the system be changed?", but "How will the change come about?"

The most sane and practical way to get the machinery of measurement and accountability into motion is jointly, with corporate management in a leadership role. The arguments for this approach over government mandates would be tough to contest.

First, a body of experience and expertise has been developed within corporate circles. This takes in a wide range of methodology, from the techniques of definition, analysis, measurement, and evaluation to information management and dissemination. The tools are at hand. We have only to use them.

Second, business is ideally tooled up to initiate change because of all segments of society it is the one most accustomed to coping with change. It's common knowledge that the most successful corporations today are the innovators.

I am talking about new products and technologies, new concepts of marketing, production, and management.

From the standpoint of organization and operation alone, no segment of society approaches the magnitude of change imposed upon American corporate enterprise over the past two decades. Certainly not big government, which in too many instances is still mired in the bureaucratic maze of the thirties and forties. Certainly not the nation's health, education, or penal institutions.

By its inherent nature, business must adapt to change in order to survive and initiate change to flourish. The virtual demise of the autocratic executive is evidence of the change that took place in business during recent years. Today in the typical large corporation major decisions are rarely handed down as ivory tower mandates. Rather they are formulated after interdisciplined idea exchange. This is the same approach that must be used to develop meaningful social measures and reports.

Such an approach would satisfy not only men and women moved by conscience, but the hardheaded cynic as well. I refer to the tough-minded businessman who echoes Milton Friedman's philosophy as the only one that makes sense. You will recall his pronouncement made in 1970:

"In a free-enterprise, private-property system, a corporate executive is an employee of the owners of the business. He has a direct responsibility to his employers. That responsibility is to conduct the business in accordance with their desires, which generally will be to make as much money as possible while conforming to the basic rules of the society, both those embodied in law and those embodied in ethical custom."

I believe that the last two words of Mr. Friedman's statement, "ethical custom," are particularly noteworthy. It is precisely to these words that my proposal is addressed. The ultimate effect of a fair and practical system of social measurement and reporting would be to more clearly define, standardize, and upgrade ethical custom. It would make social responsibility not only fashionable, but financially beneficial as well. And it points up that social irresponsibility is unprofitable and foolhardy.

As the last century drew to a close, a reporter questioned William H. Vanderbilt regarding the adverse effects of his policies and practices on the public well-being. The tycoon's now-famous response was, "The public be damned!"

It articulated in large measure the typical business executive philosophy in that unenlightened era.

Today no rational corporate leader would even harbor such a sentiment, let alone voice it. Yet under prevailing conditions, unwittingly or not, the public *is* being damned. Effective corporate social measurement and reporting may not solve all of society's problems. But it will make "public damning" by unconscionable corporations a damn sight harder.

# 2

# THE LAUNCHING PAD ITCH

There's a comfortable, convenient way for the business executive to get the social tiger off his back. It is simply to affirm the much-quoted pronouncement that "a corporation's sole responsibility is to pursue the profit objective within the framework of the law and to maximize return on shareholder investment."

Self-righteously echoing this contention, many managers breezily dismiss social responsibility as somebody else's problem and get back to the business at hand.

But if their intention is sincere, are they really off the hook? A hard look at the facts of business life and the corporate power structure in America soon reveals that they're not.

FACT OF LIFE No. 1. The main bulk of financial and manpower resources in this country are owned or controlled by corporations. Many major U.S. industries are dominated by three to five corporations. Corporate power is further expanded and tentaclized by such devices as interlocking directorates and joint venture agreements. No case is being made here against the power structure per se: its constructive potential is unlimited. But the uses and implications of power must be questioned and searched—and challenged where they run counter to the public interest.

As John Diebold points out, public concern about corporate power isn't hard to understand. "The biggest American company, General Motors, has an annual sales volume which is larger than the gross national product of all but about the fifteen biggest industrial countries of the free world; it ranks in about the same class as Australia, Sweden, the Netherlands, and Mexico. Nobody would suggest that the people of Australia, Sweden, the Netherlands, and Mexico do not need democratic governments to see that their actions are in the interests of all the people. It is therefore rather worrying that General Motors is ruled by what is nominally a shareholder-elected plutocracy, but is actually a corporate self-perpetuating oligarchy."[1]

FACT OF LIFE NO. 2. Big corporations, in their profit pursuits and at times outside their profit pursuits, act aggressively to shape and influence the laws they virtuously conform to. They "persuade" and sometimes control government officials through campaign contributions and other means. If XYZ Corporation is threatened by a proposed new bill that would impose added taxes, controls, or important restrictions, it is not unusual for the top man to inform the Democratic or Republican campaign chairman that corporate executives' contributions might depend on the way the voting goes. Nor is it unusual for the chief executive to "suggest" to division managers that they contact local congressmen and make the company position known. The congressman, cognizant of the financial and vote-getting heft involved, is quick to get the message.

Realistically, in large measure, big business is self-regulating. The laws it obeys frequently are the laws it helps to form.

FACT OF LIFE NO. 3. Corporations to an increasing degree help create many of the social ills that exist. This is not by choice or design. But inherent to our massive, complex, rapidly mushrooming free enterprise system is the inevitability of social abuses, some because they are germane to the profit pursuit, some because of thoughtlessness, a small minority the result of negligence or unscrupulousness. For example:

• Corporation A in its manufacturing processes generates a noxious effluent that pollutes the environment.

• Corporation B markets an aerosol product that, despite rigid quality controls, has been known to blow up in the face of consumers.

• Corporation C operates a factory eight miles from a neighboring slum area. No mass transit link exists between the plant and the ghetto. The only convenient means of transportation is the automobile. Thus minority residents are effectively barred from employment.

• Corporation D releases toxic waste into a nearby stream with damage to fish life and potential harm to the area's water supply.

• Corporation E markets cosmetic products in small bottles. Each unit is packed with a corrugated wrap in a small box. The small box goes into a larger box, then into a "six-pack" which includes a special liner. When the six-packs are shipped they go into cartons stuffed with filler material. The tons of waste thus produced must be somehow returned to the environment.

• Corporation F does business in South Africa and elsewhere where government policy and practice is repressive towards exploited natives.

• Corporation G distributes and lavishly advertises pharmaceutical products with questionable healing value.

• Corporation H instead of using rail service dispatches a large fleet of trucks that transports products over several states adding to traffic congestion, highway deterioration, and air pollution.

• Corporation I manufactures antipersonnel and incendiary bombs that shred human bodies and destroy acres of farmland and foliage.

• Corporation J sponsors TV commercials depicting affluent America enjoying exotic vacations. Have-not extremists viewing such scenes have emotions fanned to new heights of violence potential.

Such are the realities of corporate life. The intention is neither to judge nor indict. Business is business. And a strong case could be made for the economic consequences were these activities to cease.

Yet the reality remains. The ills of society—pollution, job discrimination, crime in the streets, traffic congestion, health and safety hazards, the energy crisis, and all the rest of it—are as much a by-product of corporate activity as any other function.

The corporation executive who states that "It's none of my business" deludes nobody but himself.

### Hopeful Signs of Progress

Many large and progressive U.S. companies are facing up to the realization that social improvement is indeed a prime corporate social responsibility in our time. Each in its own way confronts the issues as squarely, honestly, and intelligently as possible, devoting significant executive and financial resources to the task.

Yet nationwide it is a splintered and fragmented effort. True, several conferences and symposia on corporate social responsibility have been held. A host of articles have appeared on the subject. But in practical terms, methodology applied to date has been mainly hit or miss. Policies, planning, and programs vary sharply from company to company and industry to industry. There has been little coordination nationally. We find scant agreement regarding priorities, issues to consider, action courses to follow. Nor have acceptable guidelines been established to define areas of responsibility, set and evaluate improvement needs and objectives, measure progress toward predefined goals.

On one point, however, most concerned social planners, government administrators, and business executives are in agreement. GNP and other economic indicators currently in vogue have questionable value in the assessment of working and living standards in our nation and in our communities. We are in critical need of a new set of indicators and guidelines more directly and practically related to the problems at hand.

Establishing social indicators will be a complex and difficult task. It will require funding to get the job done. It will require a pooling of social and corporate talents, a meeting of minds. It will require as it did in the Apollo lunar landing project a sublimation of personal aspirations and goals and a dedication to the overriding objective of completing the task.

Compounding the problems and complexity is articulate opposition, much of it honest and well meant, to the establishment of social indicators at this time if at all. To start, we run head-on into a hard brick wall of semantics. What are social indicators? How will they be used? What are they supposed to accomplish? Widespread confusion and disagreement exists on these points.

For our purposes here I think the definition outlined in the Department of Health, Education, and Welfare's useful *Toward a Social Report* will do as well as any. In essence this described a social indicator as a direct measure of welfare. If it changes in the "right" direction, other factors remaining equal, it means the human condition has improved. A change in the wrong direction indicates the reverse.

The number of doctors, policemen, classrooms, or cells could not be social indicators.

Valid social indicators might include such items as incidence of crime in an area, good housing available, job opportunities, high school dropouts, adult school enrollment, trade school opportunities, income level, health level, amount of adequate transportation, citizens on the streets at night, health service options, number of people on welfare, alcoholism or drug addiction cases, library usage, school absenteeism, cases of vandalism, voting turnout.

Such opponents as H. E. Freeman and E. B. Sheldon, while they see some possible value in social indicators, contend it is naive to regard them as some kind of panacea. Agreed. Panaceas are hard to come by. They also point out that social indicators cannot force decisions, and cannot of themselves influence politicians or set up values and goals. Agreed.

Others argue we must know more about human behavior before attempting to establish social indicators designed to help determine and assess the human condition. Will we ever know enough about human behavior?

Still others point out that quality of life is hard to determine; it means different things to different people. There's truth in this reasoning, too. But try convincing the resident of a rat-infested building that the source of his distress is uncertain. Or try telling a terrified ghetto inhabitant that incidence of mugging is too vaguely relevant. Or try explaining to an unemployed father of five that we must wait for a better understanding of his foibles and motivations to attack the source of his trouble.

However uncertain and contradictory human needs and desires may seem, we have learned one thing from marketing research: If you ask enough people what they want and need you get a pretty good idea of the answer. Not a perfect idea, but a pretty good idea, and that's enough for a start. You can refine and improve from there.

Social indicators probably will never be as clearcut as we would like them to be. No one who has even briefly assessed the situation would deny that a great number of variable cross-cutting, and interacting factors are at play in our society. Nuclear and hydroelectric power plants, for example, cut down hugely on air pollution. And they're critically needed in many areas to shore power reliability, avoid blackouts, and provide needed reserves as energy for such items as treatment and recycling of wastes and reclamation of sewage water. But they also mar scenic beauty around mountain, lake, and river sites, conservationists complain, create danger to fish life, and in the case of nuclear plants create radiation hazards.

There's little doubt that in many cases foolproof indicators are most assuredly possible and within our reach. On the positive side, we have a great deal working for us. Much of the data we need is already at hand. Sophisticated data-gathering and information-management tools and techniques have been developed by industry and government. Extensive study and research on the subject already has been conducted.

We possess the manpower, resources, and skill to develop a meaningful set of social indicators in a scientific, logical, and organized manner as we developed economic indicators in the past. It's a matter of bringing all significant factors to bear in a multidisciplined effort, then weighting and classifying them according to the identified needs and preferences of the great mass of people.

## Only a Tool

Far cry from panacea, a meaningful set of social indicators would not even serve as a remedy. It would be simply a tool or conveyance to help with lift-off from the launching pad. Standards and guidelines, national and local, were never needed more urgently than they are today. They're essential, in fact, if we are to expect corporations to bear their fair share of the responsibility for the creation and correction of America's social problems.

Imperfect or not, social indicators would help us:

• Measure the impact of corporate actions on the quality of life, nationally and locally.

• Identify human needs more accurately than we do today and set objectives designed to fulfill them.

• Determine level of expenditures required to meet goals and plan budgets accordingly.

• Determine what data we must have to understand more thoroughly the human condition and the interacting factors that affect it.

• Pinpoint developing social problems in time to take corrective action.

• Determine which social programs might best serve society and, once established, help determine their progress and usefulness.

• Develop a Socio-Economic Operating Statement (SEOS), or perhaps even a social balance sheet.

• Measure the social costs and benefits of innovations, the impacts on society of research and development, new products and plants.

• Gauge the effectiveness with which Social Administrator X as compared to Administrator Y is managing his program or job.

Finally, and perhaps most important, it would help Administrators X and Y to know how well each is doing on an ongoing basis.

What about the distortions, the vagaries, interactional complexities, misinterpretations, and unquantifiable aspects? They will help to ensure the system's imperfection pretty much in the way the imperfection of the GNP and other economic indicators are currently ensured.

## After Good Intentions, What?

We have come a long way, but there's a big trip ahead of us. As I already pointed out, there is evidence of increasing concern in top executive suites about the corporation's role in achieving social improvement. Profit improvement still ranks as the number one corporate objective and in my opinion always should. But more and more businessmen, stirred by conscience on the one hand and practical considerations on the other, are accepting the premise that the business of business is not income generation alone. Needless to say there is still much resistance to this concept, especially among chief executives of smaller corporations that have neither time, money, nor manpower—or so they believe—to invest in "profitless" enterprise.

Nonetheless, it is becoming clear to a growing number of

thoughtful managers that social deterioration must inevitably bring profit deterioration in its wake. Thus top management interest and involvement in corporate social action takes on added momentum each day. Several large companies already have formed planning committees membered by directors and high-level executives to define corporate policy and spell out program objectives. A handful have even gone so far as to include social action alongside of profit contribution in evaluating the performance of individual managers.

When it comes to nailing down focus and scope of social involvement, however, managers grope falteringly in a familiar morass.

The president of a large consumer products company stated the problem to me the other day. "We know that we should be expanding our social involvement and we're resolved to do it. But with what areas of activity should we be concerned? How broad should our involvement be? How large an investment are we expected to make? What way do we have of knowing how large an investment our competitors will be making? Without social indicators and uniform industry standards how can we properly measure our efforts and evaluate the progress being made? How can we compare this progress against other progress in the field?"

His questions are honest and earnest. His points are well taken. He's a conscience-driven businessman. He is also a practical executive who knows he will be held to account by his directors, shareholders, and associates for his company's profit performance.

How far should he go? Where does he draw the line?

He doesn't have the answers. Neither do I.

Certain areas of corporate involvement are fairly obvious. But when we reach beyond pollution, minority hiring and training, and employee benefits the morass grows appreciably thicker. Compounding the problem is the disparity of the social consequences of corporate activities from company to company and industry to industry.

The factory that produces metal stampings from precut

sheets is clearly less of a polluter than the oil company, public utility, or automobile manufacturer where pollution is a by-product of the business. Does this mean the polluter should bear the main brunt of the mammoth pollution control burden while the nonpolluter is absolved of responsibility?

Obviously not. The metal stamper couldn't operate without light to see by, power to run its presses, vehicles to transport its products.

General Motors, gargantuan as it is, would be forced out of business if it were compelled to clean up the air by itself. No company faced with unreasonable demands erosive of profit margins could survive for long in the marketplace.

Clearly environmental cleanup and social reform are responsibilities that must be shared by all segments of society, and the corporate responsibility must be equitably distributed among all segments of business.

Where an oil company is concerned, for example, how much involvement, how much of an investment, is fair and reasonable? Most major oil companies publicize the pollution control research they are conducting in glowing terms in company publications and the public press. They provide facts and figures, review strides being made.

But when Oilco tells the world it has just spent $1 million on an ambitious pollution control project, what does it really add up to? Possibly, taking Oilco's revenues and contribution to pollution into consideration, $1 million is a fraction of what should have been spent. Or perhaps it's a half million more than it could reasonably be required to invest.

As things stand now we have no way of knowing. It is difficult even in such obvious areas as pollution, minority hiring, and employee benefits—areas that relate directly to the operation of the business—for the individual corporation to assess the fair scope of its responsibility. In such vaguely defined areas as housing, education, health care, and crime control, it is virtually impossible.

Socially responsible managers need outside help and

multidisciplined collaboration to determine proper focus and scope. Inevitably this brings us back full cycle to the need for national guidelines and standards, equitably developed, industry by industry by expert study groups representing major segments of interest and activity.

## More Answers Needed

Today a growing number of corporate managements are soul-searching questions of focus and scope in meetings and conferences both in-plant and out. Here are some of the questions we see emerging from such sessions.

• To what extent is a corporation expected to go in assessing the social consequences of proposed mergers or acquisitions?

• Is providing added job satisfaction and fulfillment for employees to be regarded as a social responsibility or part of a company's operating philosophy?

• What about product safety? If a product is 99 percent safe, how much investment should a company be expected to make to make it 99.5 percent safe?

• How much money should we spend on our plant safety program?

• Are we exerting undue influence and pressure on legislators to pass the measures most favorable to our profit objectives?

• To what extent are we supposed to go in considering the social consequences of a proposed new product or innovation?

• How far must we go in assessing the social consequences of a new plant site or relocation?

• How can we accurately evaluate whether our minority hiring and training program is adequate or competitively unwise?

• Should our advertising philosophy and investment be revamped with the social implications taken more strongly into consideration?

34

• What degree of pollution control are we expected to shoot for? If it costs a million dollars to eliminate 95 percent of the contamination and another million to eliminate the remaining 5 percent, are we obligated to spend the second million as well?

• Are consumer and minority interests entitled to a voice in formulating major corporate policies and plans?

• How are we supposed to gauge the social consequences of our military supply programs? Is it our responsibility to pass judgment on the uses of such items as antipersonnel weapons?

• Is it our responsibility to pass judgment on the policies and activities of foreign governments, bypassing profit opportunities where such judgment is unfavorable?

• How much financial and manpower support to community programs and improvements is considered our fair share?

• Can we reasonably be expected to cut down on our product packaging at the expense of sales in order to reduce the ultimate waste that results from excess packaging?

• Are we expected to alter our transportation planning if it costs money to do so in order to reduce local congestion and pollution?

• Is it our responsibility to monitor the policies and activities of suppliers and contractors with whom we deal, to withhold business if we feel they are socially irresponsible?

• Are we expected to stop production on profitable products that are not truly beneficial to the user—such as certain cosmetics and pharmaceuticals?

• Are such functions as the rehabilitation of drug addicts and alcoholics really the business of business?

• How much financial support are we expected to give to community education and health care programs?

• To what extent is community cultural activity the business of business?

In real life, of course, we inevitably find Chief Executive A on the one hand who wants to do his part and Chief Executive B on the other hand who spots personal gain if he permits somebody else to carry the burden. So it has

35

been since the beginning of time whenever there was a job to be done. The genuinely concerned manager seriously ponders such questions as outlined above. The cynical self-centered businessman dismisses them as unworthy of his time. We need mechanisms in our system that will reward Executive A for his interest and concern and make it more difficult for Executive B to get off the hook.

Translated practically, the difference between the two attitudes boils down to corporate action that either benefits or hurts society. A's company, for example, will consider using propane fuel despite the extra cost because it significantly reduces pollution. B's company bases such decisions on cost factors alone.

A is the Xerox manager whose sense of social responsibility led to the company's granting leaves for several employees to teach retarded children, campaign for mine safety, and perform other social contributions at no loss in pay. He's the IBM manager who loaned eighteen employees to black colleges for a year's stint as "adjunct faculty." He's the Kemper Insurance Companies manager who takes pride that his company was the first national corporation to publicly announce its policy of hiring rehabilitated drug addicts. B would regard such moves as being hazardous to profits.

One of the great injustices in our society today is that in the eyes of investors, shareholders, financial analysts, and his peers Executive A is a less capable manager than Executive B because of his social conscience. Since the final arbiter in our society is the financial statement, this is simple to explain. A's expenditures decrease earnings. Unhampered by such spending, B produces better "results" in terms we all understand and measures we use to evaluate performance.

A social profit and loss statement assessed side by side with financial statements would help to reweight the scales. A network of nationwide standards, social indicators, and industry guidelines would lay the necessary groundwork for meaningful social reporting. It would constitute a major stride forward in the goal of achieving a practical payoff for socially responsible corporate action.

For one thing, a corporate social action report, picked up by the national business and general press, would serve as a potent visual tool. It would help in the structuring of realistic tax and other economic incentives and disincentives designed to encourage constructive social action. It would work toward the development of imaginative market mechanisms that would make good corporate citizenship helpful instead of harmful to the conscience-driven manager. As we shall see later in the book, a movement is already in swing to influence investor action based on corporations' response to their social obligations.

Externally audited socio-economic operating statements produced by companies across the nation would help speed the development of such mechanisms. The ultimate result could be a powerfully persuasive impact, not only on Executive A but on Executive B as well.

Resistance to corporate social involvement and research comes not only from the businessman who views his sole responsibility as the maximization of profits and corporate growth. Some executives regard current pressures for reform as heretical attempts to usurp traditional management authority. I have seen poorly concealed anger and hostility expressed by intractable opponents of change, a kind of emotionalism akin to the indignation of nobles on recalling the demise of their fiefdoms.

Like it or not, a revolution is in progress. We are a society in transition. Traditional concepts are being challenged. Change is inevitable, and in the process some fiefdoms will topple. But one thing seems certain. The organizations that will survive and flourish are not those that bitterly oppose the transition and seek to block the restructuring, but the corporations that adjust to rational change and help pioneer it.

A different kind of resistance stems from those echelons of management that are below the summit. In the well-run corporation managers are assigned milestone objectives in line with profit goals. Effective time utilization has long been a serious problem for the hardworking middle manager. Today's executive who can do his job well and at the same time avoid excessively long hours, homework, and weekend work is a corporate rarity. Understandably, some managers view the new trend toward social involvement as another potential intruder on their personal time, a source of family disruption, a threat to profit objectives. They see time and effort devoted to social programs as time and effort taken away from departmental objectives.

A key task in executive top suites occupied by genuinely concerned businessmen will be one of communication and education. On the one hand the job will be to allay middle management fears and on the other hand to make sure they're unjustified. To be truly effective corporate social programs can't be assumed on a "spare time" basis; they must be allocated the same time and importance as ordinary business activities. Just as the individual corporation shouldn't be penalized for good citizenship, so the individual manager shouldn't be penalized for his socially beneficial activities. Just as the individual corporation should be assessed by society on its social contribution, so should the individual manager be assessed by his superiors on his personal contribution to his company's social improvement goals.

Still others resist corporate social action because they fear the consequences of exposure when past practices are probed. I know of one manager who has employed hundreds of people over a period of years. He bitterly opposes the introduction of proposed hiring reforms. An associate told me why.

"The program would mean investigation into past hiring practices department by department," he confided. "He's worried to death about this. To put it bluntly, he's a bigot. I doubt that he's hired more than one percent blacks or Puerto Ricans over the past ten years. He's afraid of what the consequences might be if his record is publicized."

It's easy to argue that a bigot deserves to be embarrassed.

But our primary objective, social reform, must be kept in mind. Top management concentration should be on the future, not on the past. It should be made clear that the purpose of research and study is not to expose and embarrass, but to restructure and improve.

## Social Action Goals

In his book, *Future Shock*, Alvin Toffler writes:

> As we hurtle toward super-industrialism . . . a new ethos emerges in which other goals begin to gain parity with, and even supplant those of economic welfare. In personal terms, self-fulfillment, social responsibility, aesthetic achievement, hedonistic individualism, and an array of other goals vie with and often overshadow the raw drive for material success. Affluence serves as a base from which men begin to strive for varied post-economic ends.[2]

It's no revelation to business, political, and social leaders that meaningful goals must be set before meaningful change can occur. Before launching a rocket we must establish a destination. Determined resolve will help produce the necessary impetus for action. But good intentions alone will carry us about as far as a trolley car equipped with blocks instead of wheels. We need a good set of strong, clearly defined national goals and satellite local and industry goals more urgently today than ever before.

The question is how can we come by such goals and make them stick? Presidents Eisenhower, Johnson, and Nixon all recognized and voiced the need for them. Each attempted to have national goals framed and brought into the system. Each in turn failed. Voluminous tomes were produced outlining ambitious and lofty objectives. But they had little effect on the actions of government, corporations, and communities. Why?

One reason, I think, was the reluctance of politicians to confront constituents with unpalatable realities about the status quo. Before attempting to clean up a crime-ridden community, officials in power must admit that the problem exists. But, reasons Jones, if he admits to voters that the situation in his bailiwick is deperate, how will they react? They're likely to assume Jones is unable to control the problem, and cast their votes for Smith.

What we need are mechanisms built into the system, an objective monitoring and measurement network, that will compel a realistic airing of the true situation. The public is entitled to no less.

Another reason past attempts to set national goals have failed is that they were followed by heated and prolonged rhetoric but little if any constructive action. Here we slam into another tough hurdle. We can preach, plead, admonish, and issue lofty appeals to our heart's content. Yet expecting administrators, businessmen, politicians, and other ambitious men and women to subordinate personal aspirations and objectives in favor of the common good may be, except in rare instances, a bit much to hope for.

We have witnessed the individual power play in business, in large institutions, and especially in government where it is most visible. Smith's programs and ideas may have all kinds of merit. But his political opponent will automatically combat them as a matter of contesting expediency. Continuing controversy will rage, not with social objectives in mind but political ambition, not with human needs in the balance but potential votes. If Jones wins out, Smith's programs will be scrapped, not because they're bad programs necessarily, but because they were conceived and created by the opposition. So, out with the bath water goes a good deal of substance, and the status quo prevails. Vying for power and influence inevitably gets in the way of the truth.

Again, a social audit and reporting system would help in some measure to isolate the truth from the political hypnotics. It would aid the dispassionate evaluation of Smith's programs and Jones's programs in the light of identified needs, established social indicators, and achievement goals.

Getting back to panaceas, however, they don't exist where social restructuring is concerned. Social reporting or not, we need the right kind of additional study, research, and data to bypass the natural roadblocks confronting us. We need guidelines and controls designed to ensure non-partisan, goal-oriented decision-making and action.

What I'm talking about is a "wartime" socio-economy with Republicans and Democrats, students and business-men, social scientists and educators working in unison against a common foe—the erosion of our society's founda-tions. Our overriding aim must be to protect and preserve the basic system, philosophy, and life style which, for all its shortcomings, has for over two centuries produced the highest standards of freedom, self-determination, and abundance ever experienced by man.

Is it an achievable goal? Without question. When the United States declared war on the forces of Hitler, Musso-lini, and Hirohito all factions of our society joined together and operated in an efficient, coordinated manner to defeat the enemy. Later when we declared war on space, the same phenomenon occurred. It will occur if we wage an all-out war against the forces that today are threatening our sur-vival as a nation, potentially a more dangerous and sinister adversary than any we have faced to date.

## Roadblock Number One

When one listens to the unending rhetoric, views the dis-sension in our society, and ponders the failures to date, it becomes clear that the unifying task at hand is gargantuan and complex. How can we pull it off? What magic will we need to establish Operation Restructure as America's over-riding priority? What instruments, rules, and procedures must we introduce to marshall all segments of society toward this goal?

"At the present time," notes Arjay Miller, former presi-dent of Ford Motor Company, now dean of Stanford Uni-versity's Graduate School of Business, "we have no mech-

anism, no good way of resolving conflicting priorities. . . .
As a businessman," he asks, "what can you do about it? In
my opinion, the basic approaches and techniques that have
worked so well in the private sector are also applicable in
the public sector. Whenever a businessman is faced with a
difficult choice, the first thing he does is determine the
facts. Before he approves a new product or a new program,
he first determines how much it will cost. This approach
may sound so obvious and elementary that you wonder why
I bring it up at all. All too often, however, it is not used in
public decision-making."[3]

There's a great deal more to be done than collecting facts
and determining costs. But Mr. Miller makes a point which,
from the corporate standpoint, adds a critical dimension to
the job at hand.

It is quite simply that corporate social responsibility
involves something more than good citizenship and conscionable social behavior; it encompasses as well a vital role
in the creation of the restructuring blueprint itself. No segment of society is better organized, staffed, and equipped
than business to gather, process, and manage the vast storehouse of information that will be required for the job. No
segment is more experienced and sophisticated in the setting
of goals, monitoring of results, assessment of programs and
progress.

In addition, in America's giant multinational corporations in particular, there exists so wide-ranging a multiplicity of conflicting interests and objectives, power strug-
gles and diverse disciplines that they are in a sense micro-
cosms of society itself. High-level executives in large corporations are nothing if not coordinators and unifiers within
their own organizations. Perhaps some of this talent, training, and experience could be applied to the broader task of
national unification of purpose, which in my view consti-
tutes roadblock number one.

# 3

# THE PROFIT
# DRAG MYTH

My files include a long list of actions already undertaken by progressive corporations to improve the living condition in America. These range from crime and pollution control to better housing and education for the disadvantaged. Many of the actions benefit not only society, but the individual companies as well in the most tangible way possible. They make money on the programs. In my view, the mindless assumption that profit-making and social progress are incompatible is a grave and costly error. It is one all too easily made where top management fails to take the sensible long-term approach to corporate profitability.

The social responsibility payoff has been attested to time and again. The most patent cost justification is a simple matter of good sticksmanship—sidestepping the penalties of social irresponsibility. Innumerable top managements already have learned that the alternatives to conscience-driven corporate citizenship can be grim ones indeed. If you doubt this statement, talk with any president whose company has been the target of a crippling student or consumer boycott. Ask a high-level Dow Chemical Company executive to level with you regarding the image consequences of its decision to produce napalm. Get the reaction of a company official whose bank, office, or plant has been bombed by some misguided fanatic. Talk with a division head or general manager whose plant was closed down because it polluted the environment.

The point is clear. It's a distinct economic advantage to avoid the disruption of business.

Nowhere are the negative consequences of resistance to social pressures more evident than in the pollution control field. Under the new clean air and water amendments, noncompliance can be risky and expensive. Hence compliance is profitable.

EXAMPLE. A New England company had drums of waste matter barged out to sea. Days later they floated ashore, the company's name boldly stenciled on the side. It was hard to determine which cost was greater: damage to the company's public image, or the cost of gathering up and redisposing of the waste.

EXAMPLE. In an eastern city of forty thousand, toxic waste emptied into the sewer system destroyed bacteria being used as a basis for municipal treatment. A heavy fine was imposed on the company.

EXAMPLE. In California a plant producing an odoriferous effluent was shut down for six weeks—the length of time it took to correct the situation.

Most companies have not as yet been hit with the full impact of the new pollution control legislation. The laws are tough and getting tougher. Aside from the frightening possibility of plant shut down for noncompliance, a knowing violation can bring a $25,000 per day fine, a year in jail, or both. If the offense is repeated, the penalty may double right down the line. Added to this, citizen-action suits can be brought against polluters by area residents, a growing trend, officials report.

It takes more than PR-puffery and token "good deeds" to relieve the corporate spine of social pressures. Apart from the stirrings of conscience, it takes a pragmatic and hard-nosed approach. One enlightened chief executive informed me, "The only reasoning that makes sense to me is this: Either you expend the effort, money, and manpower needed to respond to public needs and pressures, or you invite lawmakers to take matters into their own hands. And if there's one thing the business sector doesn't need at this point, it's more legislation."

## The Opportunity Potential

The fulfillment of corporate social obligations automatically implies a responsiveness to community wants and needs. As Russia watchers can attest, when suppliers of merchandise fail to respond to market requirements, the result is storehouses filled with unsold goods.

For the farsighted management, profit performance means zeroing in on long-range consumer needs and taking steps to fulfill them. Often such action is compatible with social progress and reform.

A Bank of America spokesman, speaking on this subject at a UCLA Social Audit Conference, used the bank's student loan philosophy as an example. The simplistic cost justification approach, he pointed out, is to subtract earnings on student loans from earnings on nonstudent loans and chalk up the difference as social responsibility cost.

But a depth probe reveals that there's much more involved. Analyzing the situation with an eye to the future, there are other factors to consider. For one thing, the socially conscious corporation has a big plus working for it in the recruitment of intelligent and selfless employees. How much is this worth? How many new and loyal customers— not only students but their parents as well—might be created on the heels of a liberal loan program? What about the expansion of education in the community and the structuring of a more viable economy in which the bank will do business?

"These things muddy the water," notes the spokesman. "Just making a straight calculation as to cost is not enough."

The point makes itself. Treating socially beneficial programs as somebody else's business may produce precisely that result, the generation of business for somebody else.

Admittedly it isn't easy to assign a dollar value to intangible results and expectations. In the spring of 1973, for example, Senator Thomas J. McIntyre (D–N.H.) and Representative Silvio O. Conte (R–Mass.), cochairmen of the New England congressional delegation's Ad Hoc Committee on Oil Problems, were taken to see an Atlantic Richfield Company oil refinery in Bellingham, Washington.

New England, of course, has had a severe heating-fuel shortage and would profit by having refineries built in the area. The problem is that New England legislators have long had strong reservations that a refinery could be built clean enough to satisfy tourist-conscious New Englanders' environmental concerns.

After seeing the Bellingham refinery, however, Conte and McIntyre contacted colleagues, gushing with admiration over Arco's refinery. Said Conte: "We were impressed how ducks, fish, and wildlife seemed to thrive around the refinery and along the beach. It seems improbable, but we had to ask whether the refinery was actually operating while we were there." Both legislators in effect lobbied in Washington for the company, stating that refineries could be built that minimize pollution dangers. Conte even issued a press release telling constituents about his visit.

How does one put a price tag on such an incident, obviously the by-product of corporate social awareness? It would be no simple matter. But clearly benefits that accrue in this manner are important considerations when decisions over investments for social improvements are in the weighing process.

The benefits of corporate good citizenship are not always intangible. This is especially true when it comes to pollution control. "To hear most businessmen tell it," states a business weekly writer, "purging pollution is a costly task that will eat up capital investment funds and erode profits." At Dow

Chemical Company this attitude is greeted with a polite smile. It is thus far managing to offset completely the costs of its ambitious pollution control program.

Dow regards pollution as a wasted resource—valuable material dumped into the air and water or fed into expensive treatment plants. The company is out to eliminate pollution at the source, by changing production processes and by recycling waste streams for further processing. To date, Dow has recovered enough valuable chemicals and boosted its processing efficiencies so much that its abatement program is more than paying its way.

As Dow Chairman Carl A. Gerstacker states the case: "There's a profit opportunity in pollution prevention that we have only just begun to realize."

Dow displays this attitude regarding another area of corporate responsibility as well, the push for product safety. Discussing an expensive program labeled "product stewardship," Gerstacker flatly admits it is profit-motivated.

Product stewardship presumably assumes full responsibility for the way its products affect people. It takes special pains to ensure that products will have no adverse effect on either the environment or consumer. Gerstacker categorizes the program as a powerful marketing tool. "If we do a better job of product stewardship than our competitors," he reasons, "it will be recognized in the marketplace."

Of course efforts of this kind add to the cost of the product. As one Dow manager points out, there's always the "little guy" who wants the "cheapest product he can get," toxic or not. Where this occurs, it becomes the salesman's task to convince the customer that the safer product, even if more expensive, will cost less over the long pull.

I believe that a growing trend will soon become apparent. That is government's increased role in helping to make corporate social action more financially attractive. Imaginative new incentives will be developed to offset investment costs involved. This will be most visible where corporations deal directly with government on a customer–supplier basis. In short, a company's social improvement contribution—or its lack—will increasingly serve as a key factor in the awarding of government contracts.

I think we will also be seeing a new mix of spicy tax advantages of the kind granted to foundations that meet the requirement of disbursing a fixed percentage of their assets annually. In much the same way companies making significant voluntary contributions to social improvement will get tax breaks to help offset the cost.

When incentives are factored in along with intangible benefits relating to image, loyalty, and morale, cost-justification of social actions will in many cases be sufficient to pass the scrutiny of even the most cost-conscious business executive.

## Compatibility Analysis

Today most companies are pretty much in the dark regarding consumer preferences and expectations. They're not sure how the public views the corporation and its role in the community. Nor are they clear as to what portion of corporate expenditures comes under the rubric of social improvement and what goes under the mantle of business operating expense.

All this already is altering. It will change even more in months to come as management's effort to evaluate social contributions scientifically expands and refines. The new approach will be apparent most of all in the selection of corporate social resource allocations where alternatives exist.

It will not apply where inexorable social pressures force corporate action. If Tactless Operating Corporation, for example, finds itself with a riot or strike threatened because it refuses to hire and train minority workers, no real choice is present. It's either reform or shut down. There's nothing to analyze, no alternatives to weigh.

Compatibility Analysis, as I call it, is the management

process which determines how, on the one hand, corporate action can serve to meet social objectives and, on the other, derive maximum corporate profitability from the program. It represents a growing trend ideally illustrated by the Dow Chemical example previously described.

A typical situation where Compatibility Analysis might apply is where medium-sized Corn Pad Manufacturing Company has earmarked the hypothetical sum of $50,000 for investment in community social improvement. Proposed involvement narrows down to three favored choices: (1) sponsorship of a local symphony orchestra group; (2) contribution to the National Conjunctivitis Drive; (3) support of a parklands restoration project.

To which of these three worthy causes should the company contribute money, possibly lend manpower assistance as well? In the past, most corporate decisions of this type were based on a combination of the chief executive officer's pet interests and preferences and the selling talents of the fund-raising campaigner. In the future, such decisions will be based more on the best corporate payoff potential as determined by managerial investigation and sound business judgment.

I see nothing to fault this philosophy and approach. Compatibility Analysis is a relatively straightforward process. Facts and hard data are available in every community. Informed judgments can be made, if not with foolproof accuracy, with at least fair assurance that the social action chosen is one that will provide maximum exposure and return for the company in terms of better employee, customer, and investor relations.

Ideally, of course, by-product benefits would serve to offset the cost of social investment. These could accrue in the form of recovered wastes from pollution control installations, consulting fees generated as a result of expertise developed in a particular area of social endeavor, the development of new technology leading to marketable products or services, and the like. One major electronics company, at last report, appears on the verge of initiating a whole new division whose function will be to assist other companies in the task of setting up waste treatment facilities and programs.

But new marketing opportunities are not the only ones that, over the long pull, produce corporate revenues. No sophisticated manager needs schooling in the practical value of good public relations.

Getting back to our hypothetical example, assume that a probe into the feasibility of contributing to the National Conjunctivitis Drive discloses that the local share of national moneys collected would be negligible. Thus specific community benefits, recognition, and appreciation would be slight.

Symphony orchestra patronage would produce greater exposure and good will, thereby yielding a larger return on investment. Still, interest in this venture, while spirited, is relatively limited in the community. The parklands restoration project, on the other hand, is of overriding concern to a great number of families in the area according to press reports, local officials, and projected figures. Comparative studies reveal it would fulfill more human needs than either of the other alternatives and would receive the greatest play in the press and good company identification. From a return on investment standpoint, parklands participation would be most compatible with corporate profit objectives.

Will this kind of analysis act to starve less compatible but much-needed programs? It could. Unless imaginative incentive devices—government-, foundation-, and community-initiated—can be built into the system to add exposure and recognition, provide special tax breaks, or in other ways offset the lower return on less popular programs.

I observe a growing trend for the equivalent of Compatibility Analyses evaluations prior to finalizing corporate social action programs and plans. In some cases, the information pipelines necessary to make social investment value judgments are adequate to provide management with at least a ball park estimate of comparative benefits. But clearly we have a long way to go before truly informed and intelligent social resource allocation decisions can be made in the corporation, in the community, and on the national level. And the pressures for better social reporting and more effective measurement yardsticks are just as clearly on the rise.

## *Output Yardsticks Needed*

"How much money would you estimate your company invested in social action programs last year?"

I posed this question separately to three high-level executives of a nationally known corporation in the East. The answers I received were in wide disagreement. It is apparent that notions about what does and does not constitute corporate social contribution varies considerably from manager to manager. Nor is this situation unique to the company in question.

If a municipal mandate compels installation of an expensive pollution control device, is this a social contribution? If an equal opportunity ruling forces a company to increase minority hiring, is this a social contribution? Or is it only a social contribution if the action is voluntary, unforced by law or business need? Opinions will differ, depending on the individual with whom you are talking.

That confusion exists on such issues will be confirmed by any manager who has wrestled with the problem. Yet despite the muddlement, disagreements regarding social action inputs will prove relatively easy to resolve. The problem, in fact, will pretty much resolve itself in time as definitions and guidelines start to emerge out of the corporate social audits so clearly in the offing.

More difficult to come by, I fear, will be the kind of meaningful measurement needed to gauge social action outputs or results. The importance of such measures cannot be overstated. Corporations will require them as key decision aids in determining whether to continue and/or expand existing programs, and/or break ground on new programs. Communities will need them to properly evaluate the effectiveness of programs in force and of promotional and fund-raising efforts. The federal government will need output measures in the evaluation and setting of national social priorities. How much foreign aid is feasible, for example, in light of our own poor and underfed populations in Appalachia and other regions at home? Value standards do not currently exist to adequately deal with such questions.

As Virgil B. Day, General Electric Company's vice president of business environment, points out: "Managers must set goals and objectives for institutional change, and they must be measured in part by their performance against these goals."

He adds, if managers are expected by the public and their own top management to factor a new set of considerations into their planning and decision-making, it will be self-defeating to continue measuring their performance by obsolete, narrow criteria.

It's significant and encouraging that GE and several other large progressive corporations are attempting to include in their measurement systems meaningful elements for the purpose of assessing managerial performance in the area of equal employment opportunity. On a broader scale, Day advocates installing the machinery of "human assets accounting" that would hold managers accountable for their handling of human resources in the same way they are currently held accountable for physical resources. What it boils down to, quite simply, is the kind of measurement by which top management and the board of directors can effectively audit the corporation's total social performance.

A handful of the nation's larger corporations already are setting up plans and forming study groups to ponder and soul-search such undertakings. But frontiers being explored are new and unfamiliar. Blueprints and road maps are critically needed along with investment equalizers and fair share technology. In the university, association, foundation, and other intracorporate dialogues that will inevitably proliferate in the months to come, more will be accomplished in a shorter period of time if we can succeed in burning off the semantic fog that presently enshrouds corporate social enterprise.

It appears clear to me—and to experts I've discussed this with—that a framework of socio-economic audits and reports, nationally standardized and refined on an ongoing basis, would bring all players into the same ball park under the same set of rules. With common denominators established to properly relate and assess input and output factors, the conscience-motivated concepts of social management will in time become as pragmatically functional as the profit-motivated concepts of marketing or financial management are today.

### The Noble Rhetoric

THE PRESIDENTIAL PRONOUNCEMENT. "We must take every step in our power to assist minority businessmen in their efforts to become independent and self-sufficient."

Yes, but how effectively does this company succeed in putting its money where it will count?

THE PRESIDENTIAL PRONOUNCEMENT. "The business sector has no less a stake in cleaning up the environment than any other segment of society."

Yes, but is this company doing all that it should and could be doing to control the pollution stemming from its own manufacturing process?

THE PRESIDENTIAL PRONOUNCEMENT. "School dropouts constitute a shameful waste of precious human resources. They are also a menace to our safety and well-being. As corporate leaders it is our prime responsibility to see that as many of these people as possible are trained, rehabilitated, and put to work."

Yes, but does this company's hiring and training policies properly regard school dropouts as potentially convertible assets, or as productivity hazards to be avoided?

At this point there is no real way of knowing. The problem is that corporate actions don't always match voiced sentiments in eloquence and inspirational content. Another prime function of reliable measurement would be to separate the lip servers from the people servers for all to see.

Businessmen and their critics alike agree that such traditional indicators of corporate success as the balance sheet and profit and loss statement have an incomplete bearing on the modern corporation's good citizenship rating. Few executives would argue that for profit performance to be properly evaluated, a structure of goal-directed indicators and guidelines is essential. A similar structure is no less essential if we're to assess corporate social performance with any degree of accuracy.

## Questions and Answers

As a consultant to management I know that when you ask the right questions, problems have a way of resolving themselves. Questions are a consultant's main stock in trade. He rarely offers concrete advice or suggests a course of action to follow. Those intimately involved in the operations under consideration are better qualified than he is to come up with the specific actions needed to correct operating and organizational malfunctions. His task is to pinpoint the problem areas through the questionnaire technique. It's the most simple approach in the world, and it works.

Surely there is no shortage of pertinent questions in the social sector. Take the subject of unutilized or underutilized human resources alone. How much could the value of these resources be improved by educational investment? Through the successful rehabilitation of drug users and alcoholics? Through the reduction of disease in a given community?

What social costs are attributable to broken homes in the community? In what reportable ways would the community benefit through effective crime control? If $100, $200,

$300 would have to be added to the price of an automobile to convert it into a nonpolluter, would society benefit enough?

What about the social value of corporate investment designed to make work more interesting and individually fulfilling? Suppose the cost of making a deadly boring job more enjoyable were a 10 percent cut in pay. Would the employee be willing to accept it?

How much would it cost society to take meaningful action in such areas as those outlined above? How much would it cost society if we continue deferring such action?

No one would pretend that the answers to such questions are easy to come by. But given adequate research and analysis—a fraction of which is already under way—the answers are attainable. We have come a long way in the past two decades in mastering the intricacies of information accumulation, processing, and management. We have produced the hardware and technology needed to break down the data and structure it into a practical system of measurement guidelines and indicators that will gradually improve as refinements are built into it.

As I view the problem, we are concerned with three types of measures primarily: (1) Micro socio-economic measurements—these deal with straightforward issues that relate to individual corporations, such as pollution control or minority hiring. (2) Macro socio-economic measurements—these take in the whole economy; they include questions about the performance of entire industries. Thus some level of organization larger than the corporation, such as the federal government, must deal with macro problems. (3) Issues involving nonprofit institutions—schools, prisons, welfare agencies, and so on.

To work on all three levels, it is vital for individuals in the various disciplines to revamp and decompartmentalize their attitudes. We already have learned in a substantial sampling of programs and projects that business executives and professional accountants can benefit from social scientists, social scientists and administrators can gain important new insights from professional accountants and business executives. We all have much to contribute to one another. The difficulty is not with the capability but with the communications required.

The first misconception I would like to dispel is the notion that waiting for norms will somehow refine the state of the art and present us with magic solutions. Had we waited for comprehensive standard costs to maintain effective business controls, we still would not have them. The same philosophy applies. We maintain controls through comparisons. Comparisons are as readily available in social enterprise as they are in everyday business practices.

A great deal of social information is already at hand. The outer boundaries of corporate social responsibility will undoubtedly be drawn in time, if indeed such boundaries exist at all. For the present, as I view it, the most logical place to get started is in those areas which relate most directly and incontestably to the activities of the business. First, there is the "work itself" and the work environment. Second, there are the production processes and their effect on the environment. Third, we have the impacts on society of the products or services offered.

Turning again to the questionnaire technique, a battery of pertinent questions suggest themselves in regard to these three basic areas. For example: Is worker compensation adequate to fulfill basic human needs? Is sufficient opportunity built into the system to ensure career growth where warranted? Are hiring, training, and promotion contingent on employee productivity potential, or do prejudicial factors like religion and skin color influence such decisions? How do employee fringe benefits—health insurance, retirement plan, recreation, holidays, child care, transportation, etc.—compare with the rest of industry?

Regarding production, are noxious vapors and other wastes discharged into the environment? To what extent does the manufacturing operation tax government facilities? Does the product use constitute a safety hazard to consumers? Can proven and discernible benefits be ascribed to the product? How much garbage and waste do the product and its wrappings inflict on the environment?

Much of this information is already available. Much more could be made available with comparative ease. Once this is accomplished individual corporate measures, comparisons, and social reporting would follow as natural by-products of the system.

## Story That Needs Telling

Granted, much of the information that is available, and much that with proper effort and investment could be made available, is not easily expressed in numerical terms. But a spate of techniques for reducing qualitative factors to quantitative form already have been developed and, with study, more will evolve. Never before have we so urgently felt the need for more precise, objective, and reliable methods of evaluation and reporting the corporation's response to its social obligations. Application, internal and external, would serve for one thing to differentiate between corporate actions that are profit-motivated and those that are motivated by the needs of society.

Most corporate social contributions are convertible in terms of the dollar. But new disciplines and techniques will be required to make the conversion. That means a radical switch from conventional methods and that's where the hard wall of opposition is most commonly encountered. In some instances an element of educated guesswork and interpretation will enter the picture. This is no easy pill for some cost accountants, analysts, marketing executives, and other businessmen who were weaned on hard data to swallow. Yet, conceding the obvious advantages of hard data over soft data, it merely underlines the importance of getting on with the task of setting up standardized guidelines and indicators. The sooner this is done, the faster the interpretive aspects will begin to diminish.

What Bank of America President A. W. Clausen once

dubbed the "arithmetic of quality" is an admittedly elusive concept. "It's a frustrating area to work in," a bank spokesman agrees, "but we are going to keep after it." The lack of data, he adds, is not deterring the search for social involvement opportunities. "It's the future we're thinking about, looking toward the day when companies will have to present hard figures on such activities."

That day is not far off. When it inevitably arrives, a by-product benefit of immeasurable value to businessmen will accompany it. To America's Great Cynical Majority, from what I've observed, U.S. corporations and their leaders compete for the Grand Prix of Scoundreldom with political malefactors of the Watergate ilk. They still believe that profits are excessive and that social contributions are a shade more than nil.

In addition to operating a viable economic unit that gives employment and produces material goods, what of the innumerable social programs, manpower, and financial contributions that most large corporations and many smaller corporations honestly participate in? To the TV-inured cynic this amounts to little more than a thin porridge cooked primarily for show. Stockholders, customers, the public—even the company's own employees and middle management in many cases—in general have a distorted view of management's true motivations and philosophy.

Communications has been repeatedly pinpointed by knowledgeable observers as the private sector's most deplorable and damaging shortcoming. Little wonder. When it comes to social involvement in particular we lack the vehicles of communication urgently needed to get the corporate story across with a degree of conviction. Certainly conventional financial statements have proven themselves inadequate to do the job. Publicity releases, dividend notices, annual reports? They receive small exposure on the one hand, credibility pains on the other.

Make the required social data available. Establish nationally standardized social indicators and measures on an industry by industry basis. What inevitably follows would be new vehicles of communication that would tell the corporate story objectively and convincingly.

## *Take the Payoff Out of Social Irresponsibility*

For each company that merits praise for its strong corporate conscience, others deserve a public lambasting for their indifference to or sidestepping of social responsibility. Conscience-stirrings or their lack occur for a variety of reasons, some pragmatic, others provoked by the innate morality of high-level executives.

• Obviously the more visible a corporation, the greater will be its motivation to have customers and the public think well of it. Consumer products heavily advertised on TV and in other media decline in sales on the heels of adverse publicity. Hence a GE or Westinghouse would have a larger stake in the feedback from its social actions—or failure to act—than XYZ Foundries which produces castings for industrial use.

• Medium- and small-size corporations are less in the national public eye than the bigs. Their actions and omissions individually have less impact on over-all society and, unless exceptionally flagrant or bizarre, might be less likely to backfire to the company's detriment. Yet it is only fair that the costs of social improvement and restructuring be equitably shared on a prorated basis by all business organizations. It's not reasonable to expect the big visible corporations to carry the nonvisibles and smalls.

• Large corporations can better afford, and are better equipped, to get into the social responsibility business in a professional manner. They're in a position to employ skilled managers whose sole function it is to monitor the company's social involvement, the impacts of its products and decisions on the community and environment. For the small company, in fact, the costs of professional investigation and analysis alone could well exceed its fair share of contribution.

• Finally, an abundance of high-level managers believe —or try to convince themselves they believe—that earning money is a corporation's sole justification for existence. They make clear to their aides that activities that distract from this objective are unrealistic and not to be tolerated. In short, these are society's corporate free loaders. They're no fonder of riots, strikes, and pollution than their social-minded counterparts. But to their way of thinking, "letting George do it" means, quite frankly, more immediate short-term profits on the bottom line.

What it boils down to is that we cannot reasonably or realistically expect to achieve nationwide corporate social responsibility on a voluntary invisible basis. Inevitably, when volunteers are called for, a handful respond, the majority remain mum.

This underlines the importance of pressures within our society that force companies large or small, visible or obscure, to contribute their fair share of the social reform cost. There are two ways to exert such pressures, one peaceful and orderly, the other violent. Of one thing we can be certain. If we don't opt for peace, we can be sure to get violence. We've already had a bitter taste of what can happen—boycotts, strikes, annual meeting disruptions on the one hand; riots, bombings, snipings, burnings on the other —when the emotions of desperate men and women are sparked to the point of explosion. That's one kind of pressure.

Well-ordered visibility and pressure can be considerably more effective and a great deal less painful. What I'm talking about is organized coordinated attention to social irresponsibility—on the causes of urban decay; unacceptable work environment; unequal standards of hiring, training, and promotion; unsatisfactory land management; air and water pollution. It could be a powerful way of countering the all too common managerial attitude that equates social responsibility with softheadedness, the myopic kind of vision that focuses exclusively on one place only, the bottom line of the current earnings statement or budget.

In my view socio-economic measurement and reporting, nationally standardized, could exert a sufficiently strong influence on corporate policy to take the built-in payoff out of social irresponsibility. Even the smaller, less visible company, if branded a social dodger by impartial reviewers, would tend to respond positively to improve its image. It would seek to avoid incurring employee, customer, and public disfavor. If it did not change its ways conscionable investors would steer clear of its securities. Local officials would be reluctant to confer special favors and cooperation. Conceivably, tax disincentives could even be worked into the system specially tailored to impose penalties on social responsibility shirkers.

Confronted by such pressures, even the relatively small minority of the more socially irresponsible chief executives would be compelled to think twice before finalizing a decision to "Let George do it."

# 4

# ACTION VERSUS MORE CONTEMPLATION

Innumerable articles, booklets, and books about corporate social responsibility have been written. Countless speeches have been delivered on the subject and pronouncements made. Yet remarkably few inroads have been accomplished to date. A key reason is that no one as yet has come up with a generally accepted definition of just what socially responsible behavior entails. Nor has anyone yet developed a measurement and reporting system officially endorsed by major segments of our dichotomous society.

As any management consultant will confirm, you can't attack a problem until you know how to measure it. An important obstacle blocking the nationwide adoption of corporate social audits is the controversy over the term itself. As so often occurs when forward movement grows critical, we find ourselves running a treadmill of semantic philosophizing.

"Social audit," as applied today, is a frown-provoking umbrella that covers in a vague way the assessment of any and all corporate activities that have an impact on society. When it gets down to such specifics as what activities are to be audited, how they are audited, and by whom, the rhetoric swells in proportion to the confusion that's generated. The phenomenon is by no means uncommon. It is historically evident any time a major transition passes through its evolutionary throes.

One reason for the wide disparities is the diverse interests and motivations existing from group to group among our nation's youth, labor movement, consumerist faction, disadvantaged citizenry, various minorities, and within the business segment itself. To the consumer advocate "social audit" might imply a tough, police-type monitoring of corporate activities with strong penalties imposed for bad marks. The receptive corporate chief prefers to think of the social audit as a device to help give visibility and perhaps shape and influence managerial decisions.

The word "audit" itself in the context of social actions is objectionable to many businessmen. If it were feasible to accomplish, I would urge that the term "social audit" be dropped. Its broad and confused use today tends to obfuscate what corporate social responsibility is all about. An audit is an examination and verification of accounts and records, no more, no less.

G. Robert Truex, Bank of America's executive vice president for social policy, believes that all we are interested in at this point is a genuinely informative report of social performance that should be at least as useful as the multitude of reports now generated on other aspects of performance. He would like to see the kind of information developed that would be useful to a chief executive in shaping policy and making crucial decisions where societal ripples are involved.[1] Others, corporate managers among them, feel this does not go far enough. And at this point we become embroiled in the internal–external hassle, a king-size roadblock in its own right.

A General Motors spokesman echoes disapproval of the term. Audit, he says, implies looking backward. The essential thing is to look forward. In 1970 GM formed its high-level Public Policy Committee, which reports directly to the board. The committee considers such matters as automotive emission control, automotive safety, research and development, mass transit, the company's relations with the insurance industry, and GM's position on a host of public issues. It deals with the taking of initiatives and setting of priorities beyond what corporate leadership might deem germane to the managerial function. In short, activities extend beyond traditional concepts ordinarily conjured up when the word auditing is used.

Certainly the social audit—whatever label emerges—if it is to be effective in helping to upgrade the corporate conscience, would be far removed from the concept of auditing as it currently applies to business practices. Critics who find the term confusing, misleading, or pejorative may have a good point in deploring its use. Over the long haul the objective of the procedure is to evaluate corporate response to the nation's social priorities. Any term that succeeds in clarifying this purpose and dispelling reservations would be all to the good.

But in the final analysis, whether we stick with "social audit" or opt for "social performance evaluation" or whatever, the label is secondary. What really counts is to get on with the job.

### The Counterattack

Evidence shows that those who are deeply concerned with getting on with the job are meeting, and will continue to meet, with some tough, determined resistance. The road ahead is strewn with potholes, hurdles, and gullies. The opposition lined up against pressures and proposed strategies for corporate social responsibility, while much of it is selfless and sincere, can at times seem formidable.

This should come as no surprise. Opposition was equally or more fierce when such innovations as the Declaration of Independence, the Constitution, and the Bill of Rights were first proposed. Later in history opponents fought to defeat such "premature" notions as the balance sheet, the profit and loss statement, the securities propectus. In fact, I can recall no time in the development of this or any other nation when a significant challenge to the status quo was not followed by a rolling storm of protest in its wake.

Change always has been and always will be the great jolter and disquieter of entrenched individuals and institutions. The admonition one hears these days from most opponents of corporate social evaluation and reporting is that we should be patient and wait. We are neither technically nor psychologically prepared for so drastic a change, the reasoned voices tell us. We're in too much of a muddle to proceed intelligently and effectively. I cannot agree with this premise.

Justice Stewart Potter once said, "I can't define obscenity, but I know it when I see it."

By the same token, we need not wait nor can we afford to wait until we can precisely set social standards and parameters. But when they are broken we know about it. No one can deny that in attempting to define and reasonably assess corporate social responsibility, a multitude of problems and questions, some of them seemingly imponderable, surface. This is to be expected. The notion that everything could quickly or easily fall into place in so wide-ranging and complex an undertaking is too far-out to consider. Of course there are problems. Naturally imponderables exist. Certainly we could not at this time, if ever, come up with standards and measures everyone would accept.

If this is the argument for deferring corrective action, we could logically rationalize postponement into the twenty-fifth century. At the risk of overstating what has become a cliché, we are living in an era of massive change which can only confuse more minds as the months hurry by. Even if by some eyeblinking magic, all the required indicators, measurement techniques, and reporting formats could be produced overnight, much of it would be obsolete by the time it was made operational. Only one fact is clear: The longer we resist pressures to fairly distribute the corporate social burden, the more difficult it will be in the future for companies to act independently and rationally to control their own destinies.

## *The Brick-Wall Opposition*

I earlier touched on the brick-wall opponents of corporate social reform. At the forefront of these are the Friedman "constructionists" who believe that the business of business is business, and that activities that do not relate to profits are none of its business. This is the basic premise used and, however shortsighted, at least it is honest.

Somewhat puzzling, however, is some of the rationale that's involved. *Fortune* writer Charles G. Burck states, for example, that "Friedman likes to dramatize his position by making the superficially shocking statement that the businessman's *only* social responsibility is to increase profits. He is against the acceptance of social responsibilities, because it implicitly expresses the socialist view that political, and not market, considerations should govern the allocation of resources, and over the long run this means reduced efficiency."[2]

Equating social responsibility with inefficiency is a bit hard to take. As Burck explains the reasoning:

> . . . because the businessman's drive for profitability is identifiable with his drive for lower costs, his profit is a pretty good measure of social welfare. Suppose two companies make similar products and sell them at about the same price. Company A nets $10 million, but Company B nets twice as much because it is run by a tough crew of hardheaded, no nonsense, endlessly striving managers motivated by abundant bonuses— the kind of men corporate critics often like to describe as s.o.b.'s. To an individual consumer, the two companies might seem to offer little choice. But so far as society at large is concerned, Company B has done a much better job, because it has used $10 million less of our resources, *i.e.*, raw material and manpower, in doing the same job. So, obviously, the s.o.b.'s have been bet-

ter for society than easygoing and irresolute managers would have been. [T]he advocates of corporate social responsibility, indeed, seem to have overlooked what may be the real case against U.S. business: It may be using too many resources for what it turns out.

The fallacy in this argument lies in the contention that the socially responsible businessman is "easygoing and irresolute." I have observed quite the contrary to be true. Most socially responsible businessmen I know are prodded by conscience. But of at least equal concern to them is the future well-being of their enterprises and their obligations to stockholders and employees. In general, and this varies from individual to individual and industry to industry, the socially responsible businessman is at least as hardheaded and pragmatic as his nonsocial counterpart. He watches costs just as closely. He pushes as hard for improved productivity. He knows he must do well in order to do good.

Nor have I ever heard anyone—from Ralph Nader to the most militant union official—propose that a company forego its stockholder dividends or operate at a loss in order to sponsor a social program or improve the environment. In fact, one of the most convincing arguments for corporate social measurement now is to establish the machinery that will prevent Company B from beating out Company A in the marketplace by shirking and shifting its fair share of profits to social improvement.

The chief difference between the socially responsible executive and his burden-shifting peer lies in the good citizen's realization that he should do something about the problems of his nation and community if he wants his company to flourish, grow, and attract good people. And he takes time out to lift his nose from the jungle of day-to-day profit-based pressures long enough to see the clearing ahead.

Another pet argument of the brick-wall opponent involves the trade-off between the cost of gathering, summarizing, and analyzing the information required to produce social audits and comparative reports and the value derived. This line falls flat because it is based on the assumption that what we're discussing are fringes and frills. Sincerely uttered, it is shortsighted and unrealistic. Brushing conscience aside, it presumes that the pressure groups fighting for action-or-else can be easily brushed aside or that they will go away of their own volition. The practical, socially responsible executive suffers from no such myopic illusions. He understands that we are arriving at a point in history where the collection and evaluation of corporate social data will be as important to a company's well-being as its financial or marketing data. He also knows that if he doesn't take aggressive action to keep his corporate conscience in line, the day is not far off when the job will be done for him.

## The Befuddled Opposition

Brick-wall social participation antagonists seek to sacrifice corporate morality at the time-battered shrine of corporate profits. The soft-line opponents, running a lengthy gamut from ultracautious to confused, present even more of a problem, comprise an even stronger deterrent to social restructuring. The main body of this segment are sincere, concerned citizens. They concede the critical need for corporate social involvement. But plunging into a fervent litany, they intellectualize the effort to death.

Meanwhile, back in the ghetto, in the industrial plant, in the pollution-shrouded city, in the prison, the hospital, the university—wherever the impacts of corporate wait-watching are felt, and that's just about everywhere—the fires of anger and desperation are being fanned ever higher.

The powder keg trembles, while the endless dialogue drags on.

LITANY NO. 1. You can't apply dollar measurement to social issues. The contention: You can't shoe-horn nonfiscal data into conventional, financial-type statements. The alternative: more research, more study, more rhetoric.

Strong arguments could be made for the contention. Dozens of imponderables could be cited to confirm the allegation that we have a great deal to learn.

How does one match costs and results on long-range programs? How do you evaluate and reflect a corporate social investment that helps an alcoholic, rehabilitates a convict, aids minority enterprise, elevates a woman or black to a management position? How do you reduce a company's safety program to cold dollar figures? Or the establishment of a nursery? How do you determine what part of the investment is social and what part is profit-designated? What part is required? What part is voluntary?

What about two competitors that set up identical minority training programs? Dollar investment is equal, but Company A is far better qualified technically and managerially to run a successful program. Should this difference be reflected? If so, how?

What happens when a company spends a sizable sum on social improvement with disappointing results? In 1967 Boise Cascade Corporation gave financial backing to a black-owned, black-managed construction firm called Boise-Burnett Corporation. The enterprise was half social, half profit. It fell on its backside because there weren't enough skilled black planners and managers in the construction business. How does one translate this social involvement in hard dollar figures?

Suppose a corporation makes a heavy social investment one year, does little in two subsequent years? How would this be reflected on a social performance report so that the company doesn't come off as a hero in year one, a bum in years two and three? Should the investment be amortized like a bond issue or capital expenditure?

Questions like these could fill several pages. No easy answers exist. But answers are clearly developable by measurement specialists and, where need be, by interdisciplinary teams qualified to produce consensus procedures on a case by case, industry by industry basis.

Analysts, accountants, and other measurement experts

already have refined soft-factor evaluation into something of an art. We have thousands of sophisticated professionals with long experience working with all kinds of social institutions and government agencies. These men and women are well into the difficulties of processing, measuring, and reporting soft data. They are accustomed to coming up with new definitions, developing new kinds of data, testing hypotheses, and structuring new theories and approaches. Admittedly we have a long way to go. But a well-stocked storehouse of know-how and savvy is already available. An impressive array of software technology is already in use, and the hardware grows more versatile and powerful each year.

When at last the job gets underway, we will have no place to go but up.

LITANY NO. 2. Why walk when you can crawl? The tendency among social-audit advocates, claim some ultra-intellectualizers, is to rush headlong into quantification however imprecisely defined the variables and imponderables may be. "The assumption," claims one, "is that a social measurement program made operational will be somehow made effective. The assumption is fallacious."

The dangers of premature quantification are spelled out in the following statement by Daniel Yankelovich: "The first step is to measure whatever can be easily measured. This is okay as far as it goes. The second step is to disregard that which cannot be easily measured or give it an arbitrary quantitative value. This is artificial and misleading. The third step is to presume that what can't be measured easily really isn't important. This is blindness. The fourth step is to say that what can't be easily measured really doesn't exist. This is suicide."[3]

The author would be correct if his assumptions were true. They are, through and including step one. I agree that the first step is to measure what can be easily measured. But I know of no measurement-now advocates who would go along with steps two, three, or four. I couldn't agree more with Mr. Yankelovich that such reasoning would be foolish, deceptive, misleading, self-defeating.

Experience shows there are a variety of ways to deal with information that is not reasonably quantifiable—narrative comparisons, value ratings by impartial experts based on qualitative standards, various methods of nonmetric scaling. Step two unquestionably is to assess the scope and significance of nonquantifiable items and work out means by which to reflect them fairly and intelligently.

Of course there's a good deal more "soft" data in social enterprise than in profit enterprise. But it's no secret that even at this late date much critical soft information is omitted from traditional financial statements. Companies furnish no information relating to management succession provisions, manpower skills inventories, product and other ideas on the burner, quality of earnings and markets, and other factors of key significance in evaluating true corporate worth and potential. If current trends persist, the day may not be far off when month-end and year-end statements will be modified to reflect such items. But in retrospect the question is: Should we have deferred the requirements for financial reporting all these years until such time as the utopian ideal could be achieved?

I think not. In this area of social evaluation and reporting it's important, I believe, to maintain an open and flexible outlook. In chapter six of this book I display and discuss a simplified model of a Socio-Economic Operating Statement (SEOS) to provide a general idea of what such a report might entail. Nonquantifiable representations are omitted since this would require extensive consideration and discussion of a technical nature out of place at this time.

The SEOS model is a basic format and makes no attempt to cope with the not-yet-refined qualitative factors. It is proposed as a launching base, or point of departure. Rigidly assessed, it may be subject to a battery of charges and challenges. What about this? Conceptually viewed, it could start fertile imaginations whirling and send thought wheels spinning. Eventually any format used as a starting base could be tailored and retailored, adjusted and readjusted to specific corporate and industry requirements so that in time the original product may not be recognizable. But the movement would be forward.

Imponderables tend to narrow down considerably and become far less formidable when related to specific companies and industries than when they are cataloged en masse in scholarly treatises or books. As evidence will soon bear out, most of the more significant corporate social activities are readily measurable in hard dollars directly, or are convertible to hard dollar representation. More frequently than not, where special problems and exceptions exist, they carry small relative weight when balanced against the whole. Where such items are significant, the last thought that would enter the measurement professional's mind would be to ignore them, treat them arbitrarily, or pretend that they didn't exist. On the contrary, they would be duly considered, evaluated, and accounted for as they already are in countless social institutions whether corporate involvement is present or not.

LITANY NO. 3. We don't need outsiders to teach us morality. At first blush this point is well taken by many conscience-driven executives, most likely by a majority of them. A subsequent chapter will deal in some depth with the internal–external hassle. But the gist of this argument, often resentfully expressed, is that a company's top management is at least as well qualified as outsiders to assess its social responsibility on the one hand and its capabilities to fulfill it on the other. It thus stands to reason that the policy in some high executives' suites is first, that corporate social evaluation indeed should be given top management priority; and second, the audits performed—by whatever label they're called—should be strictly internal, provided primarily for the use and guidance of the company's chief executive.

Understandably, top executives are mistrustful and wary of self-appointed business critics and gadflies who make unreasonable demands and exert irritating pressures. As one president recently confided to me while discussing a brash and outspoken consumerist, "If I did what he wanted we'd be out of business in a year, hundreds of people would be thrown out of work, millions of investor dollars would go sloshing down the drain. If I worked around the clock, I couldn't think of a more socially irresponsible action to take."

And he's right. But however valid such reasoning may be, it is not all that simple. For one thing, no one with an even mildly rational approach to this problem would suggest that corporate management abdicate its right of decision or judgment to dissenters or anyone else. More important, the particular chief executive referred to happens to be a highly principled individual with a deep sense of morality. He takes proper action as he views it to satisfy himself that his company bears a fair share of the social load.

But without guidelines and standards to go by, how could an executive, however well meaning, know whether his company's social investment is large or small, fair or unfair? Without proper measurement, monitoring, and reporting, how could he gauge the investment of his two or three closest competitors? Suppose one or more of his competitors stick rigidly by the axiom that the business of business is business. What happens then? Every social dollar his company expends becomes a deduction from the bottom line of his own profit and loss statement, and indirectly, a boost for his unprincipled competitors.

On the other hand, corporate social evaluation, uniformly and impartially applied, would to the maximum degree possible put every businessman on a fair and equal footing. We may never reach this ultimate ideal. But if we start heading in that direction, it will constitute a long stride that should have been taken a long time ago.

### The "Good Guy" Factor

A decade ago a corporation could opt to invest in social improvement or not. That choice is rapidly diminishing. A decade ago corporate chief executives well might have been divided into "good guys" and "bad guys," those who were conscionable public citizens and those who vetoed any kind of move that did not add to profits.

We still have our good guys and bad guys on the corporate scene. But the realization among thoughtful businessmen is rapidly growing that the bad guys are bad for their companies as well as society, and in the long run that social irresponsibility will cost more than it saves.

Alice Tepper Marlin, executive director of the Council on Economic Priorities, puts it this way: "Corporations *are* involved. We've no choice about that. My point is that they should be held accountable for their impact on the quality of life. The U.S. government and the investing, working, and consuming public should be provided with sufficiently precise and comparable information to form a basis for evaluation."[4]

For anyone still harboring doubts about the voluntarism myth, I could cite numerous examples to point up the narrowing choice of large corporations when it comes to social involvement. In the main, companies can still determine specific actions to take. Theoretically, if chief executives so wish, they could hold fast to the hard-line laissez faire doctrine. But this is becoming harder and harder to do in big companies especially. The squeeze is on. Corporations are responding, and only in part because they feel morally obligated to respond. They're responding because a failure to respond would prove too costly in terms of bad customer and employee relations, and investor, labor, political, and environmentalist repercussions.

General Motors Corporation stands as the classic example. Demands on the world's largest industrial organization have been pyramiding in recent years. The Project on Corporate Responsibility wants GM to eliminate advertising and model restyling to finance a crash program to produce a pollution-free car. Consumer crusader Ralph Nader, backed by Justice Department lawyers, wants GM to divide into a number of independent companies to foster more competition. The Episcopal Church wants GM to lead the attack on apartheid in South Africa by refusing to do business there. The company has no intentions as of this date to accede to these demands, but it has been responding vigorously to what it deems to be "legitimate" social requirements.

GM's Public Policy Committee, which aggressively soul-searches matters relating to the corporate conscience, has already been described. In 1971 the automobile-maker became one of the first major industrial corporations to elect a black man, the Reverend Leon Sullivan, to the board. He has joined church groups in attempting to persuade the company to get out of South Africa if apartheid isn't ended. GM also named a six-man Science Advisory Committee of leading scientists and hired as vice president an air pollution expert to deal with matters environmental. Today some 15.3 percent of its work force and 3.2 percent of its salaried employees are from minority groups, up sharply over recent years.

Some critics publicly affirm that all of this is too little too late and that GM social innovations are essentially cosmetic. If the company's claim that it is indeed highly responsive to its social obligations is valid, it would be well served, I believe, by a system of social audits and reporting that objectively and impartially makes clear to the public what the true situation really is.

GM, while a prime target of social reformers, is by no means alone. As *New York Times* writer Marylin Bender notes:

> Public interest groups are pressing a record number of proposals for corporate action at the annual stockholder meetings that are now beginning. But at the same time the corporate social-responsibility movement is broadening its tactics. As specialized public-interest groups proliferate, coalesce and sometimes bicker, corporate challenges are increasingly taking a legalistic turn. Lawsuits are being filed. Petitions are

75

being made to government agencies that regulate corporations and industries.[5]

More and more companies are being challenged on more and more issues. What's more, they are being investigated, evaluated, and publicized by special interest groups that are often hostile. How much more effectively it would serve both the business and public sectors if evaluation and reporting could be nationally accepted and based on a carefully formulated framework of social indicators that would take all governing factors and viewpoints properly into consideration.

Nor is it group pressures alone that make the concept of voluntarism impractical. "One trouble with leaving good deeds up to individual executives," observes Gilbert Burck,

> is that not all of their companies are equally prosperous. Now that the Kaiser empire is in trouble, for example, Edgar Kaiser is taking a hard line on demands for "responsibility" in his companies. "Not to husband resources," Kaiser says with considerable feeling, "would be special irresponsibility of the highest order." Hard-pressed companies obviously cannot undertake the social programs supported by companies with strong market power, such as utilities (whose regulated rates are based on costs). And healthily profitable companies like Standard of Indiana and CNA obviously have a great advantage over companies that are constantly battling to stay in the black.

Social reformers often give better marks to companies with unique motivations to promote their public image. Levi Strauss & Company, the informal apparel and youth-ware maker, is an outstanding example. The company contributes 3 percent of its net after taxes to carefully chosen social programs, does substantial minority hiring, finances minority suppliers, and sets up day-care centers for employees' children.

Laudable as this activity is, says Burck, the company obviously gets a good deal for its money. "It does business in an intensely liberal city and has a market in which tastes are heavily influenced by young people. And so, whatever its top executives believe in their heart of hearts, their social-responsibility outlays would appear to be rather effective public relations. So far as an outsider can determine, these outlays cost no more than would conventional high-pressure public relations in a different kind of company."

As things stand now, corporations are either good guys or bad guys at least from the public viewpoint, depending on the visible social actions they take or their lack. However constructive, if a company's social action is less visible, it gets marked down. If it's struggling for survival and lacks the dollar and manpower resources for what uninformed outsiders might regard as critical action, it gets black-eyed. If its prime motivation for social action, directly or indirectly, is profits, it gets higher marks than the corporation that contributes less socially because there is less profit feedback, but nevertheless contributes its fair share or more.

Ideally, all such factors should be taken into consideration, fairly evaluated, and fairly reported. Experience teaches us that attempting to approach this ideal by relying exclusively on individual corporate initiatives is neither realistic nor practical.

## Self-Serving Selflessness

Clearly the developing trend among concerned businessmen—concerned about both their enterprises and the society in which they live—is toward what is most commonly referred to as "enlightened self-interest." This hangs on the proposition that if a corporation seeks to shirk its fair share of social responsibility both the corporation and society will suffer. The philosophy stems from changing public opinion and growing activist and political pressures on the one hand, and on the other from the stirrings of executive conscience and a growing awareness of the positive benefits to be derived from responsible corporate action.

The executive vice president of an expanding national corporation remarked to me the other day: "A whole new vista of exciting business opportunity is in the process of unfolding. I wonder how many businessmen understand what is happening."

His eyes glowed with excitement as he said it. Expanding on his comment, he reeled off a rundown of fields that "must inevitably grow," as he put it, as a result of the surge of corporate social involvement he predicts for the future. Among them were education and housing, manpower training and development, transportation, health care, and urban development, not to mention a host of new industries and occupations being spawned by the new environmental standards.

"Imagine the market potential," he exclaimed. "It should add a whole new dimension and thrust to the nation's economy."

Excited or not by the prospects, what's a corporation to do in response to the challenge? How far is it expected to go? The Committee for Economic Development poses some searching questions in this regard:

• What is the appropriate scope of corporate social involvement from the standpoint of management—considering the limitation of company resources, cost-benefit ratios, and good judgment about balancing the primary needs of the business with efforts to help improve social conditions?

• What is the appropriate scope from the standpoint of society—as judged by the comparative advantages in getting social problems dealt with by business corporations and by such other institutions as government, education, labor, private foundations, and volunteer groups?

• How much of the task can corporations undertake on an essentially voluntary basis under prevailing market conditions, and how much will need to be facilitated by changes in the governmental rules that govern the economic system?

• How can the social performance of business be evaluated?

"Clarification of these issues," notes the CED,

> would help society understand what business can reasonably be expected to accomplish, and how it can best be done. This could forestall exaggerated public expectations that corporations somehow can and should solve most of the country's social problems, and thus prevent a backlash of resentment when business performance falls short of unrealistic expectations. Conversely, clarification would facilitate the process by which business could find its optimum social role in a rational fashion. This would minimize the dual danger of underresponse and resulting public dissatisfaction, or of overresponse which could lead companies well beyond their competence, bring about destructive rivalry rather than healthy competition with other institutions, and stretch corporate capabilities so far as to sap performance in the mainstream business.

What we need, in short, is a thinking out and working out of what yardsticks, what functional areas, what measurement strategies are required to accomplish the purpose outlined above.

As some large corporations view the situation, the social audit is no great departure from accustomed procedures. Several companies already find it necessary to monitor both their people and their activities from the standpoint of social performance, not merely for public relations reasons or in response to social mandates, but for much the same reasons nonsocial staff functions are established. As one chief executive tells it, "We're encountering no particularly devastating problems. It is essentially a matter of adding a handful of staff personnel and providing some top-level guidance so that they can work out the details."

## *Age of Malaffluence*

We are living in an Age of Malaffluence. The United States and other modern nations maintain an elaborate system of economic indicators. These help gauge the state of the economy, tell us the speed and directions of change, tip us off as to how and when to apply the checks and controls needed to keep the economy healthy. Essentially, the message transmitted by these indicators is that we're living in a period of unprecedented affluence and growth. The GNP keeps rising, prospects for the future look bright, individual incomes are high, and the possession of material goods per capita is at an all-time peak.

The data may be statistically accurate as far as they go. But it's like riding a merry-go-round with the horses missing. The economic indicators reveal useful information about the physical wealth of the nation. But they fail to define the state of its intellectual, spiritual, and psychological health.

A rash of information pipelined from sundry and various sources reveals that intellectually and psychologically our society leaves much to be desired. The malaffluent input discloses wide-ranging and deep-rooted job dissatisfaction among industrial workers. It evidences the disenchantment of youth, the divisive alienation of various ethnic and economic groups, and chronicles dismal failures of our educational, penal, and health care institutions. Supportive of the information is a history replete with the consequences of disappointment and frustration ranging from riots and strikes to demonstrations and boycotts. As one former U.S. cabinet member states the case: "Gross national product is our Holy Grail, but we have no environmental index, no census statistics to measure whether the country is more livable from year to year."

A prime national priority is to address ourselves to this issue. Which brings us back where we started, to quality of life measurement and evaluation.

An oil industry vice president I know, highly moral, socially responsible, shakes his head dolefully when this subject comes up. He confesses, "I'm at a loss how to effectively define in this pluralistic and divided society, what a 'reasonably prudent, modern, socially conscious management' would be expected to undertake."

How does one assign individual responsibility for performance? How can a company determine what social areas to attack?

It has been wisely suggested that a good place to start is with activities that are easiest to quantify. These cover a rather wide and comprehensive range. Social research conducted by S. Prakash Sethi, of the University of California at Berkeley, indicates that the following corporate social activities offer the greatest promise for early quantification and measurement.

- Aid to arts and cultural activities.
- Aid to higher education and health-related activities.
- Employee-related activities: improved benefits, equal opportunity in promotion, participation in job-enrichment programs, self-development programs, job safety, the right to dissent, and encouraging participation in political activities of the employee's own choice.
- Community-related activities: local fund-raising campaigns, executive time devoted to improving the efficiency of various local governing and planning bodies, urban development, and inner-city programs.
- Minority groups: hiring, job training, development, and promotion; and encouragement of minority-owned enterprises through loans, technical assistance, subcontracting, and purchasing.
- Consumerism: product safety, product warranties, adequate consumer information, fair pricing policies, nondeceptive advertising, and complaint handling.
- Political activities (external and internal) such as taking a position on war, apartheid, etc.; supporting public-interest legislation on such issues as gun control, strinissued periodically along with conventional financial and

gent antipollution laws, better standards for consumer protection, and mass transit.

• Restructuring of corporate organization: inclusion of minority groups and other public-interest representatives on the board of directors, federal chartering of large corporations, etc.

Just think how far along the road of social progress we would be if all of the problems related to all of the items on this list could be solved.

What about the rest of the items? As noted earlier, other techniques have been developed, are being developed, and will be developed to deal with them. With regard to long-range social activities, for example, accountants already have advanced past the pioneering stage in the area of budgetary projections. This is less predictive in nature than it is a confirmation of the logic and assumptions involved. Truly qualitative evaluation of this kind is long overdue. When it is nationally implemented and refined we will find the methods and means to prepare and report the results.

However useful numbers may be, they are often misleading as is the case with national income and gross national product figures. We need to get more deeply into the measurement of human attitudes and expectations, satsifactions, and frustrations.

The city of Dayton, for example, with the support of the Kettering Foundation, has created a public opinion center to survey the attitudes and perceptions of Dayton citizens. The data collected are made publicly available and the community is learning how to use the information in its decision-making functions. Established in 1970, though still highly experimental, the center represents an encouraging step forward.

Many businessmen, social scientists, government leaders, and academicians have articulated the need for measuring and reporting corporate social activities. But observations run pell mell in a host of directions. In my view, the biggest mistake we could make at this point would be to attempt to design techniques geared to the total satisfaction of all dimensions. It will be years before social measurement can be refined to the degree that we can apply it with the relative confidence with which economic barometers are used today. When that day comes we will have done a great service to the public at large, both the private and nonprivate sectors, the dissenters and the dissented against. The greatest service we can do now is to help expedite that event.

# 5

# SOCIAL AUDIT:
# THE STATE
# OF THE ART

A small but growing number of large corporations are experimenting with social audit programs. Many more are quietly attempting to assess their own social performance. "The majority of companies listed in *Fortune's* Top 500," notes the head of a firm that specializes in preparing annual reports, "discussed some aspects of their social involvement in their 1972 reports." This is up more than a third over 1971.

Does this indicate increased sensitivity to, and concern about, the corporate conscience? Perhaps. But frank information exchange on the subject isn't always easy to come by. It's not surprising. One paper industry executive told me recently off the record: "I must confess that probes of this kind do not always show up the company in the best possible light."

Others are concerned about leaking proprietary information to competitors or calling their actions—or failure to act—to the attention of regulatory agencies or consumerists.

An oilman notes cynically, "Corporate articulateness regarding social issues tends to increase as the heat gets turned higher. But most revelations to date are internally generated backslapping to boost the corporate profile." Indeed, as data revealed by the Council on Economic Priorities and others make clear, companies that are the worst social offenders strain hardest to broadcast "good deeds" in an effort to offset unfavorable publicity. Thus, as of this writing at least, social reporting is still largely a public relations function.

Yet increasing numbers of high-level managers are coming to the conclusion that formal social audits are clearly in the offing. These men and women are working hard to develop corporate guidelines to help them assess the social implications of business decisions, define areas of social concern and practical limitations of involvement and investment. They further recognize that for social audits to evolve constructively rather than restrictively, cooperation between profit and nonprofit sectors is essential, that the alternative to business initiative is pressure-group-induced legislation.

### How to Get Started

Most businessmen understand the crucial here-and-now need for increased corporate social responsibility, formalized and organized on a nationwide basis. It is a hopeful sign, I believe, that the majority have consciences that match their understanding. In my judgment, the will to improve society exists. It's the initiative that's lacking. Many are apprehensive and reluctant about taking the first step. Others ask, "How do you get started?"

If it were a financial or marketing program at issue they would not ask this question. My answer is you get started on developing a social audit and reporting program the same way you would get started on any other corporate program or function of top-level priority. You start with a plan grounded on the premise that social needs and business needs are inextricably laced together. First, you spell out as specifically as you can how the corporate conscience rates today. You establish the direction in which you are headed now, and to the best of your ability the social objectives you have in mind for the future.

In view of today's accelerating pace of change and expectations of super-acceleration in the years ahead, planning inputs must be sufficiently broad to cover all contingencies and encompass all alternatives that might help you to accurately assess the social implications of your company's business decisions and policy formulations.

Some companies, to their everlasting credit, are striking out, however gropingly, in this direction. A handful already have begun to take imaginatively aggressive action along these lines. General Electric Company for one has probably come as far along this road as anyone. Its strategic social planning is being built on a foundation of four major cornerstones—social, political, economic, technological. Step one in GE's planning process is the development of a long-term environmental forecast. This will serve as a gun sight "to make explicit the environmental assumptions upon which all corporate strategies—marketing, manpower, technological, financial, and social—will be based."

Developing this long-range planning tool in 1972, nine "tunnel visions of the future" were considered. These dealt with probable occurrences in the international, defense, social, political, legal, economic, technological, manpower, and financial sectors of corporate involvement. From the hundreds of specific trends and events pinpointed in these nine segments, the company identified about seventy-five that had the highest combined weighting of probability and importance; in short, those that are most significant so far as General Electric is concerned.

The advantages of the environmental analysis as a launching pad approach? In terms of defining corporate social policy, the company notes, the utility of this analysis lies in: (1) making explicit *all* the environmental assumptions on which corporate planning and policy-making should be based; (2) integrating the "social" factors and the "business" factors into the planning framework; (3) confronting future corporate problems as a system of interrelated issues and pressures (*i.e.*, seeing them as a piece, rather than piecemeal), with all their attendant complexities and trade-offs; (4) identifying the spectrum of probable future constraints *and opportunities* for corporate performance; (5) providing an opportunity, early in the planning cycle, for determining needed corporate responses to changing conditions.

General Electric's Ian H. Wilson underlines the importance of incorporating significant new dimensions of risk and social criteria into the strategic planning process. "If society is going to evaluate corporate performance against a broader set of criteria," he notes, "it surely makes good business sense for management to ward off future problems—or to seize anticipated opportunities—by building these criteria into its own strategy evaluation process. The fact that there are no simple, quantifiable answers to such questions certainly complicates the task; however, it in no way diminishes the need for it."

A number of major corporations already appear to be taking this cue. A leading food company, having concluded that corporate social audits are destined to become widespread in the foreseeable future, initiated its own strategic planning with an ambitious corporationwide "social inventory." The purpose of this information-gathering effort is to define, in numerical terms if possible, what is currently being done, to spell out current social policies, and to pinpoint and clarify existing social goals. This, states a spokesman, should help us to "ascertain what we are now doing and to help us plan what progress we should expect in selected areas."

He views the social inventory as an essential first step toward ongoing social audits, but stresses that the *initial* inventory is *not* intended for public disclosure. If this does come, it would come later on the heels of much more experience.

To get the project underway the company organized a Social Audit Task Force in the winter of 1972. Included were several department heads and corporate vice presidents from such areas as planning, legal, tax, financial, community relations, accounting, and investor relations. In retrospect, notes the spokesman, the task force should also have included representatives from one or more operating divisions, personnel, and minority or women employees.

In developing the inventory, the task force tried to identify what society expects of the company. Significant impact areas were placed high on the list, low impact areas deemphasized. In general, the inventory broke down into three major sectors: (1) public, (2) consumer, (3) employee. Items under "public" included charitable giving, composition of the board of directors, recruiting of women and minorities, and ecology. Under "consumer," advertising, consumer complaints, product safety, packaging, and labeling were among topics listed. And the "employee" category included pay and fringe benefits, employee safety, and responding to the employee voice.

Responsibility for planning and conducting the inventory, designing the basic questionnaire, evaluating replies, and following up on questionable answers was invested in the task force group. The data, supplied by twenty "monitors" in appropriate staff departments, was processed by the accounting department. The resultant report took four months to complete.

Among conclusions reached, notes the spokesman who prefers for his company to remain anonymous for the present: The inventory was tougher to conduct than originally anticipated; definitions, sometimes fuzzy, constituted a major problem. Another problem was getting people to define the "social" part of their jobs.

On the plus side, most people very willingly participated. But expressing results in meaningful terms was not always easy. Nor was it easy to pose the right questions in the right way.

The spokesman also stresses that written replies are wholly inadequate to do the inventory job; face-to-face interviews and follow-ups are essential. Particular difficulty was experienced in splitting the "social" from the "good business" part of various activities, especially those in the consumer segment of the business.

*Spreading Clouds Over Mist*

Another point made by the spokesman just cited is that his company's inventory was "not intended to evaluate the benefit of our actions."

I believe this to be the only sensible approach to take. Too much has been made of the input/output hassle, with some debating that social contribution should be measured in terms of success, not investment.

Harvard Business School's Raymond A. Bauer and Dan H. Fenn, Jr., state:

> Cost by itself is an inadequate measure, since the main question the company will want to answer about each activity is, "Was it a success?" The difficulty in anwering this question is that corporate activities can ordinarily be measured only in terms of such intermediate effects as the number of people who have received a given type of service—say the number of community residents whose apartments have been rehabilitated. Few social programs can satisfactorily document what the delivery of these services did for the people who received them.
>
> In addition, these activities are extremely expensive to evaluate, and it is doubtful whether any company would find it feasible to make frequent evaluations of its total contributions. A compounding difficulty here is that the answer to the question, even if one gets it, may be valueless. If a company ascertains the number of high school students who use the computer it has donated, what has it really learned? Probably, not very much.[1]

Linking success measurement to the corporate social audit and report, in my opinion, serves to confuse the issue and delay the launching. Needless to say, the achievement of social improvement objectives is what we're all shooting for. I think we can also assume that an integral part of a company's social involvement would be to take whatever steps are needed to maximize the chances of success. But at this time to insist on incorporating into the appraisal of the individual corporate conscience qualitative measurement and evaluation of results is unrealistic and self-defeating.

Suppose, for example, that Company A lends a $40,000-a-year executive to a poverty program and that Competitor B lends a $40,000-executive to the same program. Suppose further that Company A's man might be judged somewhat more expert than the other fellow. Does that mean Company A has shown a higher degree of social responsibility than Company B? Attempting to make such a judgment would be taking an easily quantifiable social effort and needlessly shrouding it with intangible nonquantifiable factors.

Or suppose that two GI's, Tom and Ben, are recruited into the army during a national emergency. Presumably it is the responsibility of each to serve his country to the best of his ability. But suppose Tom, immediately after being shipped to the front, is killed by a land mine, and Ben, who is fortunate enough to survive the ordeal, succeeds in killing enemy troops. Does this mean that Ben, who was successful, fulfilled his obligation more responsibly than Tom who, having died, was unproductive at his job?

It's what one *puts into* a task that is the critical element in determining responsible action and behavior.

The point might also be made that as corporate social involvement proliferates, the system of national indicators and standards that will inevitably evolve along with it will include guidelines designed to help managers distinguish between strategies that work and strategies that fail. Placing undue focus upon output results measurement at this time, I believe, would be permitting the caboose to control the speed and progress of the train.

## Setting the Stage

To successfully develop and implement a social audit and measurement program, a company must be organizationally geared to the effort. It must prepare itself structurally to set into motion corporate machinery to (1) evaluate, quantitatively where possible, the social environment in which it functions; (2) establish improvement objectives; (3) make fair-share resource allocations in response to identified needs; (4) measure and evaluate corporate social involvement on an ongoing basis. However formidable this may seem it's no more complicated than setting up the planning and support organization for a new product line, a marketing or manpower development program.

In setting long- and short-range goals to achieve predetermined social gains, it will mean formulating procedures to deal with public and internal pressures, existing and anticipated legal restraints.

Most companies already embarked on social improvement programs attack the problem from two separate flanks. Supergoal number one is to "eliminate the negative." This means addressing oneself to the question, "What are we doing that adversely affects the environment or society?" Are we damaging the ecology? Are our products useless or unsafe? Are our hiring practices discriminatory? Are work assignments mindlessly dull and dehumanizing? Is the opportunity ladder decrepit and shaky?

Supergoal number two aims at "accentuating the positive," making corporate social contributions on the premise that an improved life style in the community makes for a better, safer, and more profitable environment in which to live and work.

How can these supergoals be achieved? Some interesting concepts already have been devised. Others are in the process of development.

## *"Perceived Reality" Approach*

Any plant designed to manufacture a car totally devoid of defects, a cookie box that could never contain a broken cookie, a TV set that couldn't fail, an aerosol can guaranteed to work flawlessly 100 percent of the time, would be prohibitively expensive. It would not be practical, realistic, or beneficial to society to tool up for absolute perfection of our products and services. This is an elementary fact of business life. But try telling it to the motorist with a broken water pump a hundred miles from home, or the TV viewer whose picture turns to snow as the best actor award is about to be announced, or the consumer whose almost-full spray deodorant refuses to spray when she's late for a date. From the standpoint of the fractional minority of product defect victims, the producer is heartily cussed out. In short, from the public's point of view *real* performance and *perceived* performance do not always coincide.

It applies not only to product performance but to social performance as well. And so far as a company's public profile is concerned, say advocates of the "perceived reality" approach to corporate social involvement, what matters most is not the social situation itself but the public's perception of it. The objective therefore is to attack social ills not so much from the social scientist's point of view but from the marketing analyst's point of view.

A utility executive informed me frankly, "It's our job to respond as the public expects us to respond. It's the only way to keep from being crucified."

This view implies a continuing evaluation of public attitudes regarding corporate activities inside and outside the plant. Companies already traveling this route conduct public surveys and polls—or have outsiders do it for them— to keep a steady finger on the public pulse. Survey respondents include consumers, employees, legislators, students, minority and environmental representatives, investors, etc.

The aim is to analyze existing and potential pressures and to respond as efficiently and economically as possible to relieve them. Theoretically, this could go so far as to involve advertising and other communications designed to alleviate fears and resentments real or imagined, and cool public tempers. In addition, the company operating along this line attempts to gauge its social ranking on an ongoing basis as compared with companies of equal size and scope within the industry. If it receives reasonably high marks the assumption is that the brunt of the pressure—and adverse marketplace effects—will be borne by competitors.

The lure of this approach is obvious. It's one way, or so it would seem, for a company to "get off the hook" so far as its public profile is concerned, to minimize the amount of flak flying its way. Nor is the concept lacking merit. Often the more public expectations are met, the more improvement results.

However, undue emphasis on this approach helps to perpetuate the situation where public perceptions are distorted due to inadequate information, shortsightedness, or propaganda generated with the purpose of distortion in mind. It narrows the degree of discretion a company can apply in planning social contributions and resource allocations over the long-haul basis.

### Optimum Response

Optimum response advocates seek to use the corporation's resources and capabilities in fulfilling its social obligations regardless of what public perceptions might be. The goal is to get to the root of real human needs in their proper order of priority. The customary starting point, as discussed earlier, is the inventory of activities current and projected that have impact on the social community within the company's sphere of operations.

A key tool of the optimum social responder is the social report. A proposed format of this report, which would be

earnings statement—the Socio-Economic Operating Statement (SEOS)—is displayed and described in the next chapter of this book.

A much-publicized form of social report produced by a
consulting firm to reflect its own activities is patterned after
the conventional balance sheet. To summarize briefly, it
lists under *Social Assets Available*, figures pertaining to such
subheads as Staff, Organization, Research, Public Services
Consumed Net or Tax Payments, and tallies on the bottom
"asset" line Total Social Assets Available.

Under the "liability" side of the statement, headed by
Social Commitments, Obligations, and Equity, appear
Staff, Organization, Environmental, and Society's Equity
figures, which wind up with the bottom line balancing
figure of Total Commitments, Obligations, and Equity.
This social balance sheet seems an unnecessarily cumber-
some and complicated approach, and it is not clear what
the significance of the results are even if it were practical to
prepare such a statement for most businesses, which I
doubt.

Critics of the optimum response approach point to such
familiar pitfalls as low credibility stemming from PR-ori-
ented focus on "good deeds" while conveniently playing
down unfavorable data. They declare it is not always possible to differentiate between those activities that are socially
responsible and those that are not. They further dispute the
feasibility of dollar measurement and certain quantification, and perpetuate the hassle over input/output
evaluation. Considering the present state of the art, these
arguments are not without some validity.

Over the long pull, however, it brings us once more to the
urgency of developing national standards and guidelines.
Hacked out on an industry-by-industry basis this will help
companies sort the apples and pears from the oranges and
plums, standardizing the system so that company comparisons will be simple and practical. As this comes about the
above-cited arguments will gradually run out of steam and
evaporate.

### Performance Audits

"The proper way to conduct a social audit," notes a high-level manager charged by his chief executive with the task of developing a viable program for his company, "is the same way any other effective management audit might be conducted."

He would begin by posing the key question: "Are objectives being met as projected and are they being met on schedule?" Admittedly, confesses this manager, his attempts to get such an audit under way in his company thus far have failed.

The problem doesn't lie with the concept. It lies with the shortage of standards and guidelines. Basic management tenets have long attested to the importance of clear standards relating to all functions of the business. No modern corporation could operate production, research, marketing, or any other kind of activity competitively without proper guidelines to keep costs and performance under control.

The executive cited above states the case: "Social enterprise requires the same sound management principles as business enterprise to make it work. The sooner we wake up to this fact, the more inroads we'll make into social improvement."

In some areas—pollution, safety, hiring, and others—where national guidelines are being spelled out, important social gains have been made. It appears inevitable that as guidelines are further refined and expanded into new areas of social activity that the prognosis for appropriate social audits will gradually improve.

### Process Audits

Harvard's Raymond A. Bauer and Dan H. Fenn believe that the social audit is more productive when executives sit down to examine what they are doing and how they are doing it. The most useful strategy for arriving at these answers, they contend, is the process audit. They claim management and those concerned are less interested in social achievements chalked up than how hard their company is trying to fulfill its social responsibility. Process audits would get information to management so that it could decide how the company is doing.

Simply stated, the process audit breaks down into four basic steps: (1) Assess the circumstances under which each social program audited came into being. (2) Spell out the program's goals; state in clear and concise terms what it's supposed to accomplish. (3) Explain the rationale involved —how the company plans to attain the goals, why its proposed set of actions will achieve them. (4) Describe what is actually being done as opposed to what the rationale says ought to be done.

In a nutshell, the aim of the process audit is to assemble the information that will make it possible for a management executive to assess the program. The executive can then decide whether management agrees with its goals, whether the rationale is appropriate, whether the actual implementation promises to do the job required.

In a process audit a company reflects its social contributions only, but should we also not consider a company's harmful social actions and nonactions? With militant monitoring groups and government agencies increasing in number, size, sophistication, and resolve, in my judgment we have no choice but to properly give visibility to both the pro and con social activities.

Increasingly day by day the gathering army of sharp-eyed watchdogs are reporting corporate activities in their own terms and from their own frames of reference. Even the most hardnosed manager will concede his company would be better served telling the truth about its social actions, negative or not, than have uninformed reporters airing the story for them. As one hot-blooded environmentalist flatly states: "Companies that try to conceal their socially irresponsible activities will sure as hell find they'll be dredged up and exposed."

*96*

Why process audits if we thereby ignore social detriments? Why process audits if they are used only for internal purposes and the findings are not even made available to the public—to the society for whom the social actions are being undertaken? Bauer and Fenn put it this way: For one thing, it will serve to get the show on the road.

Also, the foundations for future auditing will have been laid. The nucleus of an auditing team will have been trained. The controller will have had his first taste of the problem of assessing the true costs of social programs. Management will have a realistic basis for estimating what an audit costs and is worth. Hopefully, the fears of corporate executives will be surfaced and assuaged. To the extent that management thinks it desirable, it can build expanded ambitions into future audits. The very fact that management has undertaken an honest, systematic effort will be a plus.

In my judgment, from every indication corporate management is being forced to move beyond this hesitant half-step. Beginner's tools are available for us to move forward more positively.

### The A.R.A. Program

It is a hopeful sign that several large corporations, however fumblingly, already have undertaken or are in the process of initiating social audit programs. One interesting example is A.R.A.Services, Inc., a $700 million enterprise engaged in supplying food services to industrial plants, institutions, and airlines plus a variety of retailing and merchandising operations. In the spring of 1971, A.R.A.'s board chairman appointed a committee to investigate how well the company was meeting its social responsibilities. The groups included the corporation's executive vice president, a graduate business school dean, the chief executive of a major operating subsidiary, and the president of a management consulting firm, a subsidiary of A.R.A.

After exploring vast amounts of literature on the subject,

the committee identified six major areas of corporate social responsibility and arrived at preliminary judgments about the company's performance in each. No profound conclusions were developed from the audit. But it did provide a significant base from which to examine and evaluate the corporate role on an ongoing basis. The six major areas were as follows:

- employment and training
- environment
- consumerism
- business concern
- provision of socially needed services
- fixing responsibility within the corporation.[2]

In large measure it would appear that the A.R.A. audit was a soul-searching exercise. Under "employment and training," for example, the basic premise was stated that, "Business is increasingly expected to provide jobs and promotion opportunities, as the individual's merit dictates, to all the minorities who have historically met obstacles—the blacks, the long-time unemployed, women, the physically handicapped, and ex-convicts."

The committee then goes on to question how many disadvantaged should be found in a work force of a thousand people. How much and what kinds of training represent a conscionable (not an economic) offering. How many blacks, women and others should be advanced and to what degree in the hierarchy?

Finally, an attempt is made to evaluate with fair objectivity the company's performance: "In comparison with other companies," the committee notes, "A.R.A.'s employment and training practices measure up reasonably well," and it cites specific actions in support. Yet the tentative conclusion is reached that "by evolving standards which emphasize the rank attained by blacks, women, ex-convicts, and the physically handicapped, A.R.A. may not yet be rated 'passing.' "

Similar observations and judgments are made in the

other five areas. Reference is made by John J. Corson, president of Fry Consultants and the committee's spokesman, to the large volume of waste materials introduced into the environment by the company's vending machine installations and periodicals distribution returns. He discusses the company's moral obligations regarding the marketing of cigarettes, dealing with both the health hazard problem and the effects of this function on the sale of A.R.A. products, the company's ability to recruit, and good will generated.

The examination further raises questions about corporate contributions to social institutions in the community. How is "fair share" evaluated? It deals with the feasibility of day-care centers and other services beneficial to society. How much investment is enough; how much is too much? The review also attempts to induce A.R.A. executives to assess the extent and value of individual voluntary contributions. Are they sufficient in the light of society's expanding expectation of corporate behavior?

The social audit, at this stage in particular, must of necessity leave numerous questions unanswered. But as Mr. Corson states, "It does suggest that executives and directors have an increasing need to know about aspects of corporate operations that have received little attention to date. It also suggests that a thoroughgoing social audit will undoubtedly uncover unsuspected vulnerabilities that will demand attention in the years ahead."

It is much to the company's credit that it stands ready to honestly and willingly air its social obligations and responses. In the final analysis, such frankness and concern could only act to benefit the corporation from the standpoint of employee, customer, and public reaction, despite negative actions and omissions that are publicized. After all, virtually all companies are offenders as well as improvers in one area of social impact or another. But how many are honestly willing to soul-search their weaknesses as well as their strengths?

### Getting Down to Priorities

At this point in the development of social corporate concern and the absence of adequate qualitative standards, the measure of a company's efforts in quantitative terms in responding to its social responsibilities is significant—both internally and from the standpoint of public visibility—and there is no need to wait until new output standards are invented for social programs. Unfortunately, even accepting this approach, it is not a help to management in its attempts to determine which social responsibilities come first, which are secondary, which can be disregarded altogether.

Acceptable answers to such questions aren't easy to come by. Nor is much help in sight on the horizon. The relative urgency of society's varied needs has not been calculated and isn't likely to be in the foreseeable future.

Can cost-benefit analysis provide the solution? At best only to a very limited extent. Some of the societal costs of such social ills as drug abuse might be roughly ascertained. The same might be said for environmental damage from production or consumption. But we would be dealing only with the tip of the iceberg. Much of the same limitations would apply in trying to calculate the corporate costs of transactions where funds are diverted from business opportunity programs.

Benefits to society and to business under various conditions are tough to determine. To produce a scientific and truly meaningful qualitative cost-benefit analysis, highly sophisticated accounting methodology and sociometric techniques would be involved to compute factors properly—so much so that in many instances it is likely that the cost of the costing at this time might be prohibitive.

In one relatively straightforward application based on empirical data gathered for a midwestern utility, an attempt was made to measure the social costs and benefits from installation of an electrostatic precipitator in the utility's smokestack. Four kinds of social costs were produced by the smokestack's emissions: decreases in property values, increased incidence of respiratory diseases, the "soiling costs" of cleaning, and increased property maintenance. To estimate how much of these costs were imposed by the utility, the amount of pollutants emitted in previous years had to be related to ground-level concentrations of the pollutants. Taking other variable and fixed factors into consideration, analysis was limited to soiling costs only.

Even so, and sparing you the tedium of the technical step-by-step analysis, the procedure ultimately developed was expressed in a rather complicated algebraic formula. The time and effort expended to develop the analysis is laudable indeed, and the results were of value in the application referred to. However, studies of this kind with regard to most social investment decisions as we know them today would hardly seem feasible.

Until national goals have been established and national social indicators set, the corporation must mainly rely on an intelligent assessment of the individual social impacts of its business activities and some guidance from interested citizens groups.

Once national goals and indicators have been developed it will be a different set of circumstances. Then as experience multiplies, social indicators will operate much the same as economic and fiscal indicators operate today with regard to economic and corporate policy goals.

In one aspect of corporate social responsibility at least, a company can more readily determine which areas of investment are decidedly beneficial for all parties concerned. A major thrust of Westinghouse Electric Corporation's social action program is to pinpoint those areas where the company's advanced technological know-how can be best applied to benefit society and the company simultaneously.

At Westinghouse, assumptions on both economic and social conditions are developed by seven top officers: the board chairman, two vice chairmen, and four company presidents. Significant social problems, most of them urban in nature, were identified early. The conclusion was reached that through close coordination with federal, state, and local government representatives, the company could make important contributions in the area defined and at the same time boost its own growth and profits. An initial step was to isolate such specific high-potential targets as low-income housing and pollution control and apply technology to help solve the problems that exist.

A sampling of follow-through efforts shows that the company built several thousand low-income housing units and designed a factory for the housing market. It put together a complex capability to handle pollution control problems from diagnosis right through to final construction. It did pioneering work to solve mass transit problems. It helped develop nuclear power capabilities in response to the clean air and energy crisis. It poured large sums into pioneering technology to minimize the adverse environmental effects of high sulfur coal. It set up environmental schools for government and utility people.

This does not imply that Westinghouse's only social contributions are those that are geared to reap a profit return. The company also provides educational facilities to train the disadvantaged, conducts ambitious employee development and work fulfillment programs, and contributes to a variety of other social improvement endeavors. The Westinghouse approach appears to be imaginative, aggressive, and constructive. Yet a spokesman notes wishfully, "We could use some well-structured cost–benefit analysis to evaluate our programs, and a good impartial group to help audit results."

## The Visibility Requirement

Social audits would inevitably generate social reports. Such social reports would consist of formal statements for the decision-making and evaluative use of management executives and for the study of consumer-citizen groups as well as government agencies. Informal releases would be used by the communications media. Senator Mondale and other leaders of government as well as business thinkers already have made clear that once public visibility and public forums are created, the momentum of citizen pressure will automatically speed widespread adoption. This in my judgment would encourage wholesale dialogue between business and social leaders instead of some of the thoughtless, shortsighted mutual criticism which too frequently seems to occur.

The social tool I propose to help expedite this process is the Socio-Economic Operating Statement (SEOS). It will be discussed in some depth and detail in the following chapters.

# 6

# SOCIO-ECONOMIC
# OPERATING
# STATEMENT—
# THE SUBSTANCE

The corporate social challenge has been made abundantly clear; it is apparent to any discerning observer that the pressures on business are mounting. From all indications they will continue to mount. Never before have so many social activist groups and agencies so diligently monitored corporate social response or so articulately stated their findings and requirements. So the stage is set. No intelligent student of business and society would deny these realities.

It is equally clear that the corporation's role in society has grown diverse and complex. We can no longer look to dollar profit figures alone as a measure of operation effectiveness. Because of proliferating interaction between money-making and life-style objectives, traditional gauges of corporate "success" are no longer adequate. A new dimension has been added, the dimension of morality and citizenship. This is not reflected on existing financial statements. We have no way of determining from a profit and loss statement or balance sheet the degree of corporate conscience being exercised by a company and its leadership. A new assessment vehicle is urgently needed, one that will give visibility to a company's response to its social obligations.

True, we see increasing press coverage of corporate social contributions. We see scores of U.S. companies setting up study and action groups to formulate responsibility programs. We see a growing number of corporate leaders searching their consciences and broadening their organizations' social efforts and involvement.

When it comes to matters of conscience, however, companies differ little from individuals. We find in every community a handful of dedicated people eager to give money and time to help fulfill human needs. Others do nothing and appear unperturbed by their heedlessness. It is the same with business executives. One responds to the proddings of conscience. A competitor takes the stand that social problems are none of his company's business. Or he pays lip service to responsibility in an effort to get the tiger off his back.

But here the similarity ends. I made the point earlier that under the existing system of measurement and reporting the responsible executive is penalized, his apathetical counterpart gains a fat financial edge. In Brooklyn, New York, for example, the chief executive of a manufacturing company with profits-only on his mind, recently okayed a costly advertising program designed to increase sales and profits. His closest competitor, during the same financial reporting period, generously earmarked funds for corporate aid to minority enterprise in the area. On the financial statements both outlays were reflected in much the same way—as a reduction of earnings. The public—which includes investors, analysts, employees, and customers as well as consumers—is entitled to a fairer representation of corporate social performance as well as corporate earnings performance. The socially responsible company deserves recognition for its contributions. Its socially negligent counterpart, to offset the edge gained on competitors by virtue of its irresponsiblity, should have its omissions publicly displayed.

The means to accomplish this end do not presently exist. The Socio-Economic Operating Statement (SEOS) I propose in these next two chapters has been designed to fill this gap. It is envisioned as no panacea. But prepared periodically along with the balance sheet and profit and loss statement, it would isolate from other business activities a company's socially beneficial actions (IMPROVEMENTS) and harmful actions (DETRIMENTS), thus setting the record straight for all to see.

Let me first put the SEOS philosophy into proper perspective.

A bedraggled-looking man approaches you on the street and convinces you he's starving. Touched, you give him money for food. He takes your money, buys a pint of whiskey and swills it down, thereby worsening his liver condition without abating his hunger. Does this in any way diminish your compassion, concern, or the cash value of your contribution?

The Socio-Economic Operating Statement's overriding purpose is to give visibility to corporate social improvements and detriments. It is important to keep this in mind. SEOS's chief focus is on corporate effort, on degree of conscience exercised. It does not aim to assess program effectiveness or project results of social investment into the future. The question it seeks to answer is: How socially responsible is Company A as compared with Company B?

In short, the stand I take is that if a company meets its social obligations with responsible action, it is entitled to recognition regardless of the degree of success achieved by its efforts. And although social programs are sometimes hard to define and evaluate, we will know a social IMPROVEMENT OR DETRIMENT when we see it. And in time application and usage will help standardize and sharpen our definitions as well.

If we take this simple, anticonfusionist approach, we will find that the Socio-Economic Operating Statement will be neither difficult nor expensive to produce. What follows is a hypothetical case history to illustrate how this might work.

To set the stage, we turn to Chem Products Manufacturing Company and witness SEOS planning and development in action. The fictional CPM could be any one of over ten thousand U.S. corporations.

ACT I, SCENE I

CPM, headquartered in Anytown, U.S.A., produces a line of organic chemicals, animal, bacterial, and vegetable enzymes, plus a variety of related items. Its products are marketed nationally. Approximately 10 percent of sales are outside the United States. CPM, a medium-size company, has enjoyed slow, steady growth over the past two decades.

J. L. Probity, the company's president and chief executive officer, at a meeting of the board's directors, expressed deep concern regarding CPM's responsiveness to its social obligations. The specific questions he posed: "How socially responsible are we as compared with our leading competitors? Are our contributions reasonable and adequate? Are we spending too much? What are we doing that we shouldn't be doing? What should we be doing that we're not doing?"

Such questions, Probity pointed out, were unanswerable at this time. No reliable measure existed within the company to determine the extent to which the corporate conscience was being exercised. He made the further point that pressures for social responsibility and accounting were building daily. Legislators, citizen action groups, unions, the clergy, and a host of others were bearing down on CPM and other companies in the industry.

"If we don't take steps to determine and demonstrate our fair share of social involvement, the job will be done for us by others. Personally I'd prefer to see us come up with our own assessment and report than to have this prepared by Nader-types, professional ax-grinders, and self-appointed corporate critics gazing down our throats from an outside point of view."

He concluded by proposing that a Socio-Economic Operating Statement be prepared periodically to accompany the balance sheet and profit and loss statement. Its objective would be to measure and report as honestly and objectively as possible CPM's social actions and omissions.

### ACT I, SCENE II

Probity's first move was to set up a social study group consisting of three top aides.

"Your job," he told Executive Vice President Jim Bunting, the group's leader, "is to appoint a small interdisciplinary SEOS task force committee best qualified to define and evaluate CPM's social activities. The first phase of the committee's work will be to identify for board and top management approval a list of social improvements and detriments to be included on the statement. Its next function will be to break down these items and come up with the actual costs that are socially applicable."

"That may be tough to do in some cases. Not all social factors are easily quantifiable," Bunting said.

Probity shrugged. "Nor are all business factors easily quantifiable. Quality of earnings. Goodwill. Certain aspects of research and marketing. Employee motivation programs. We'll have to rely on intelligent judgment to develop the most objective and reliable figures we can."

"Won't this present another problem?" Bunting asked. "The natural urge will be to present figures that are most favorable to the company, to accentuate the positive and underplay the negative."

The chief executive nodded. "It could be a problem if our approach and philosophy is wrong. On the one hand, we'll have to convince the committee we're shooting for objectivity and fairness. A key purpose of SEOS is to give management an accurate fix on the way the company is responding to its social responsibilities. A euphoric presentation could only distort this picture. On the other hand, if the committee acts unrealistically, the external audit group would act as a check and control."

"External audit group?"

"That's right. Although the Socio-Economic Operating Statements and exhibits will be prepared internally, they'll be audited by an outside independent interdisciplinary team in much the same way public accountants audit financial statements today. This group would have the experience, savvy, and judgment to evaluate items selected and cost factors applied."

*108*

"It appears to me that measurement, cost evaluation, and preparation of accounting type statements constitute a major part of the job. Wouldn't it make sense to have a CPA such as Don Miller at the head of this committee?"

Miller was CPM's financial vice president.

"I couldn't agree more," Probity said.

Bunting looked thoughtful. "We're talking about an internal task force. But in some social areas like pollution we don't employ the qualified professionals within the company to provide the expertise we would need."

"So we hire outside consultants to work with the committee—environmentalists, sociologists, economists—whatever expertise we require to fill the gaps."

"Won't that be pretty expensive?"

"I don't see why it should. We're not talking about a week-to-week or month-to-month ongoing operation. We're talking about an infrequent periodic review and evaluation. There wouldn't be that many hours of consultation involved."

Following instructions, Bunting formed an internal SEOS team headed by Financial Vice President Don Miller. Others in the group included a manufacturing executive with strong chemical background, an administrative vice president who was a seasoned business generalist, a personnel executive who was also a sociologist, and the company's safety director. A pollution control expert with special expertise pertaining to the chemical industry was recruited from the outside in a consulting capacity, as was a public health administrator who completed the team.

A planning and goal-setting meeting was scheduled for the following Monday.

## ACT I, SCENE III

The president and executive vice president sat in on the initial orientation meeting to help set objectives straight and clarify any confusion of purpose or philosophy that might arise. Probity took special pains to impress on the group the importance of unbiased, objective evaluation. The team's primary goal at this point, he added, was to come up with a list of social improvements and detriments to be included on the Socio-Economic Operating Statement.

The personnel man was shaking his head. "What's the problem?" Probity asked.

"I don't see how we can tag a dollar sign to all the socially related actions we take or fail to take. Let's say we hire a black supervisor, or upgrade a woman executive, clearly socially responsible actions. But how can you cost out such things? Or suppose we set up a day-care facility where working mothers can leave their children when they come to work and pick them up when they leave? It's a social improvement, but it helps business as well. It cuts absenteeism, for one thing, reduces employee turnover for another. It should make recruitment easier and ultimately result in better qualified, more productive employees. How would you display such items on your SEOS? If we give our imaginations free rein, we could point to dozens of such items."

"I'm sure we could," Probity replied. "My advice would be to deal with them as simply and directly as you can. You can do this if you don't let your focus deviate from the main objective involved. What we're trying to do is measure and report the degree of social responsibility being exercised by the company. The emphasis should be on contribution or investment, not on the consequences. Specific costs are more easily identifiable than many people realize. Take the items you cited. If it costs us no more to hire a black supervisor than a white supervisor, we're obviously entitled to no special credit for our action. In other words, we get no dollar recognition for overcoming prejudice which should not have existed to begin with. On the other hand, if in hiring a black supervisor it means we must spend a thousand dollars more to train him for his job than his white counterpart might cost, the training cost is an investment we should show.

"The same thinking would apply to upgrading a woman executive. If she's advanced in her natural progression up the career ladder, and no special costs were involved, no credit would apply. The nursery example's a good one to consider. We could complicate this all out of proportion, or treat it simply and realistically. We know the hard costs of space, construction, personnel, and other items involved, and that's what we should reflect. No law states that responsible social behavior should exclude by-product profit and productivity benefits. If the good action we take boosts employee morale, attracts more qualified people, helps lure new customers, or whatever, it's all to the good. Attempting to cost out and display such benefits as a reduction from the expenditure would be prohibitively expensive and self-defeating. We'd spend all our time haggling over what should and shouldn't be included.

"We can't be all things to all people," Probity added. "If we break down our socially related actions into logical cost components, we'll have the figures we need. Don't forget that the ultimate goal of SEOS is to provide a means of comparison so that one company's social actions can be fairly rated against another's in its industry. This will give management the answers it needs to resolve social problems and decisions. It will give proper visibility to corporate responsiveness to offset penalties currently imposed on more conscionable managements.

"As more and more companies adopt SEOS—as a defense against Nader-type measurement and reporting, if for no other reason—treatment will become more and more standardized. This will be helped along by industry associations, emerging literature on the subject, and developing social accounting practices. It will be refined further by CPA firms, consulting organizations, and others who might become involved in the outside auditing of internally prepared Socio-Economic Operating Statements and exhibits. The process will parallel the evolution of standard accounting practices as they apply to conventional financial statements. They will never be perfect. But we'll learn to live with them and make them work for us. Does that answer your question?"

The personnel executive gave a tentative smile. "For the present, but I'm sure a hundred others will crop up."

"I don't doubt that for a minute. We'll tackle them as they arise. But the first task as I see it is to get cracking on

*111*

that list of improvements and detriments. Where problems erupt, we'll break them down and resolve each on an individual basis. I like to think that we're fair and reasonable men. If our judgment gets to be shaky at times, keep in mind that it will be subjected to the scrutiny and evaluation of that interdisciplinary panel of external experts. I have every confidence that in time the Socio-Economic Operating Statement will be standardized on an industry basis and we'll be ahead of the game for having jumped the gun and helped pioneer the effort."

ACT II, SCENE I

Financial Vice President Don Miller kicked off the SEOS team's second meeting by announcing the session's objective: "To formulate a set of guidelines and rules to help the committee identify specific social IMPROVEMENTS and DETRIMENTS that will appear on the statement."

To qualify as an IMPROVEMENT, it was decided, the expenditure would have to be aimed at enhancing the welfare of either employees or the public, safety of the product, and/or environmental conditions. The move would have to be made voluntarily by the company. Items required by union contract or law were declared ineligible since they were mandatory costs of conducting the business.

A DETRIMENT, or negative SEOS item, would be charged against the company when a responsible authority brought the need for social action to management's attention but management did not voluntarily take the action required.

"Here's where we're likely to run into a hassle or two," the manufacturing executive said testily. "How do you define 'responsible authority'? If the action hasn't been legislated as yet and management believes it's unjustified, whose opinion prevails? Or where legislation is in force, but we disagree with its interpretation or scope, why should the outsider's view prevail and not ours?"

They thrashed that around a bit. Miller summed up the conclusion that the action recommended by the outside authority would have to be one that a "reasonably prudent and socially aware businessman" would respond to positively. He added, "The fact that the determination's subjective shouldn't discourage its implementation. In traditional business accounting, research, and development items, work in process inventories, allowances for bad debt, depreciation charges, price-earnings ratios, and a variety of other factors are largely based on subjective determinations."

The administrative vice president nodded. "In any case, the committee's reasonableness, prudence, and social awareness would be subject to the presumably objective critical judgment of the external audit group. And as was already pointed out, as experience develops, many of the decisions that are debatable today will be regarded as standard operating procedure tomorrow.

As the meeting progressed, several guidelines to help the committee pinpoint IMPROVEMENTS and DETRIMENTS were suggested, refined, and formally adopted. These included:

• If a socially beneficial action is required by enforceable law or union regulations, it is not included in the SEOS.

• If a socially beneficial action is required by law, but is ignored, the cost of such an item is a DETRIMENT for the year. The same treatment is given an item if postponed, even with government approval.

• A prorated portion of salaries and related expenses of personnel who spend time in socially beneficial actions or with civic organizations is included.

• Cash and product contributions to social institutions are included.

• The cost of setting up facilities for the general good of employees or the public, if done voluntarily without union or government mandate, is included.

• Expenditures made voluntarily for the installation of safety devices on the premises or in products and not required by law or contract are included.

• Neglecting to install safety devices to protect employees or the public, where available at reasonable cost, is a DETRIMENT.

• The cost of voluntarily building a playground or nursery facility for employees and/or neighbors is included. Operating costs of the unit are also included for each succeeding year applicable.

• The cost of relandscaping strip-mining sites or other environmental eyesores, if not required by law, are included.

• Extra costs of designing and building business facilities to upgrade health, beauty, or safety standards are included.

"The items we include on the Socio-Economic Operating Statement will be in part determined subjectively," Miller said. "But a standard dollar value will be applied to the improvements and detriments. These will include those which fall into the traditional accounting classification of expense items and capital expenditures. For example, the full cost of a permanently installed pollution control device, voluntarily incurred, would be reflected on the SEOS for the year of installation. The annual operating cost of a hardcore minority training program would also be reflected. To make reference easier, the totals would be expressed in Socio-Economic Management Dollars (SEM$), thus isolating all socially beneficial expenditures voluntarily undertaken.

"In time," he concluded, "additional guidelines will be developed and refined as we continue our work with the concept. But I think this will do well for a starter."

ACT II, SCENE II

Applying the guidelines set down, the SEOS committee next started targeting in on specific corporate actions to include on the statement. Several actions and omissions were listed for possible inclusion. These were considered one by one. Most of them were readily identifiable as either IMPROVEMENTS or DETRIMENTS. But predictably, regarding some items it was difficult to assert with assurance whether they qualified as social or purely business actions. Other items involved both business and social components; differ-
*114*

entiating between the social and business part of the expenditure was not always easy. A few corporate actions triggered lively debate among committee members. Did they belong on the statement at all?

One prime example was the company's recently initiated Job Enrichment Program. A stated program objective was to improve working conditions and provide employees with more independence, greater job satisfaction, and fulfillment—clearly a social benefit. Yet while social value could not be refuted, the program's overriding purpose was to boost profits and productivity by increasing worker morale. The philosophy represented a strong business trend. The program itself was sound competitive strategy. Moreover, a host of gray areas were involved. The task of isolating social costs from business costs would be too formidable and expensive to undertake.

As Miller pointed out, "A prime SEOS objective is to provide sufficient visibility to social actions to permit a company-by-company comparison within the industry. If we omit such programs, so will other companies, thus avoiding confusion while we help standardize the scoring."

The item was bypassed.

"What about the new elevator in Building Two?" the safety director wanted to know. Building Two was a two-level warehouse adjoining the plant. The unit referred to had replaced an ancient elevator that had been in operation since the plant was constructed. Several months ago the old elevator had been identified as a potential safety hazard. Since the new unit eliminated the hazard, the safety director argued, it was a social improvement. The manufacturing executive disagreed.

"Let's be honest and objective," he said. "Our main purpose in making that move was to improve materials-handling efficiency, to eliminate breakdowns and delays. It was a sound business move. On top of that, union pressure had been building to shut down that old unit. Had we ignored those demands, it would have meant inviting labor trouble. We installed that elevator because we had to; there was nothing voluntary about it."

The item was omitted.

Finally, an old warehouse building which had outlived its usefulness had been sold and a new one built to replace it. The new facility was located several miles from the old one in an area not easily accessible except by car. About twenty-five workers, mostly from disadvantaged communities, could not afford cars and were forced to resign as a result of the relocation.

The question was raised, "Does the company's failure to provide special transportation to preserve these jobs constitute a social detriment?" The decision was no. Company-operated transportation had been considered and costed out by the accounting department. It was found that the cost of transportation would be prohibitively expensive. As Miller put it, "It's an action no prudent management could be reasonably expected to take."

The item was omitted.

After a sequence of additional meetings, special studies, and consultations with outside experts, a list of social IMPROVEMENTS and DETRIMENTS was compiled and submitted to the board for approval. The board reviewed the items, deleted a few, suggested changes in the wording here and there. In short order the SEOS committee was given a green light to complete the final phase of its work.

ACT II, SCENE III

Establishing classifications for the Socio-Economic Operating Statement was easily accomplished. Social IMPROVEMENTS and DETRIMENTS, it was discovered, fell into three general categories: social actions that are people-related, environment-related, product-related. With these categories determined, the statement's headings and subheads virtually generated themselves. The end product of the committee's work was presented as follows.

### CHEM PRODUCTS MANUFACTURING CO., INC.
## Socio-Economic Operating Statement for the Year Ending December 31, 1973.

I    *Social Actions—People-Related*

A—IMPROVEMENTS

| | | | |
|---|---|---|---|
| 1. | Minority enterprise technical assistance program | $ 4,000 | |
| 2. | Emergency flood relief | 3,000 | |
| 3. | Training program for handicapped workers | 8,000 | |
| 4. | Executive time—hospital trusteeship | 5,000 | |
| 5. | Minority hiring program—extra training and turnover costs | 6,000 | |
| 6. | Day-care center for children of employees—set-up and maintenance cost; voluntarily established | 11,000 | |
| | Total Improvements | | 37,000 |

B—Less DETRIMENTS

| | | | |
|---|---|---|---|
| 1. | Postponed installation of hydraulic safety control system—cost of unit | 16,000 | 16,000 |

C—People-Related Actions—Net Improvement for the Year      **$21,000**

II    *Social Actions—Environment-Related*

A—IMPROVEMENTS

| | | | |
|---|---|---|---|
| 1. | Cost of installing water quality monitoring system to control pollution | 22,000 | |
| 2. | Cost of clearing and landscaping company-owned ravaged area and dump | 41,000 | |
| 3. | Executive time—free consulting service to state environmental protection agency | 4,000 | |
| | Total Improvements | | 67,000 |

B—Less DETRIMENTS

| | | | |
|---|---|---|---|
| 1. | Deferral of liquid waste treatment facility | 60,000 | |
| 2. | Postponed installation of higher smoke stacks to reduce air pollution | 19,000 | |
| | Total Detriments | | 79,000 |

C—Environment-Related Actions—Net Deficit for the Year      ( $12,000)

III    *Social Actions—Product-Related*

A—IMPROVEMENTS

| | | | |
|---|---|---|---|
| 1. | Voluntarily discontinued alkaline product judged unsafe for home use—projected annual net income | 23,000 | |
| 2. | Salary of chemical engineer on loan to government product safety committee | 21,000 | |
| | Total Improvements | | 44,000 |

B—Less DETRIMENTS

| | | | |
|---|---|---|---|
| 1. | Cost of process redesign to reduce manufacturing hazard—recommended by Safety Council, but implementation deferred | 36,000 | 36,000 |

C—Product-Related Actions—Net Improvement for the Year      **$8,000**

Total Socio-Economic Improvements for the Year Ending December 31, 1973      **$17,000**

Add: Net Cumulative Socio-Economic Improvements as at January 1, 1973      **$176,000**

GRAND TOTAL NET SOCIO-ECONOMIC IMPROVEMENTS TO DECEMBER 31, 1973      **$193,000**

A half page of notes was appended to the statement. This called attention to a number of corporate actions where social aspects were involved, but where attempting to isolate the social and business factors would have been impractical or misleading. The purpose and scope of these actions were indicated, social IMPROVEMENTS and DETRIMENTS described in narrative form. Following each item was a brief explanation of why it was not included in the main body of the SEOS. Among the actions so treated were: the company's Job Enrichment Program, Employee Tuition Refund Program, plant relandscaping, a consumer education program to promote the safe use of products, innovations made in the employee cafeteria, and CPM's failure to provide bus transportation to the new warehouse for employees who did not own cars.

CURTAIN

## New Perspective on the Corporate Conscience

After assessing the company's first published Socio-Economic Operating Statement, preliminary conclusions were reached by chief executive officer J. L. Probity and members of the board.

• By isolating social actions from business activities, the SEOS provides new insights into CPM's responsiveness to its social obligations, useful for internal management decision-making.

• SEOS possesses a powerful potential to provide a study base for company-by-company comparisons of social responsibility within the industry. Spurred by the efforts and cooperation of professional trade associations, chambers of commerce, commerce and industry groups, and other interested parties, adoption of the SEOS pattern and philosophy by increasing numbers of companies could occur in relatively quick order.

• Companies refusing to cooperate would be indicted as much by their refusal as by their lack of social contribution and awareness. They would be subject to strong pressures by legislators, business critics, citizen groups, and the press. In time it would become foolhardy and costly to spurn social measurement and reporting.

• The only sensible approach to social measurement is the simple approach. Until such time as the state of the art becomes more sophisticated, corporate actions so complex and controversial as to make the isolation of social aspects prohibitively expensive are best handled in narrative form. As industry guidelines and standards emerge, analyses will be easier to make, and may be represented in the main body of statements as consensus opinion decrees.

• The most important goal of the project was to make a practical start at social measurement and reporting. Probity and the board unanimously agreed that this goal was successfully accomplished.

It was further determined that the SEOS would be prepared annually at the outset, perhaps semiannually later on. In general, it would follow the publication pattern of CPM's highly formalized balance sheets and profit and loss statements as they appear in the company's annual and interim stockholder reports.

SEOS analysis in conjunction with traditional financial statements gives the reviewer two important new insights: It enables the individual to evaluate the corporation's capacity to respond to social obligations; and it permits a comparative assessment of how this capability is being used.

The bottom line of the SEOS shows an accumulation of the company's net Socio-Economic IMPROVEMENTS or DETRIMENTS to date. The statement thus periodically displays social actions for the year for the three major classifications listed, along with degree of corporate conscience exercised on an ongoing basis. It provides insiders and outsiders with comparative social data on both a current and long-ranging basis.

I am convinced that SEOS, or an equivalent social statement, will be required for most business organizations by the time the eighties are upon us. SEOS exhibits will be demanded by consumer groups, institutional investors, increasing numbers of government regulatory agencies.

To project a step further, we might anticipate "Annual Surveys of Corporate Responsibility" in *Fortune, Business Week, Wall Street Journal, Harvard Business Review,* and similar publications. Such studies in fact already have been attempted by a handful of editors. Once the trend gains momentum, there is little question it will be taken up by general publications as well—*Time, Newsweek, The New York Times,* and others. Corporate comparisons by the press would be inevitable. It does not take an exceptionally fertile imagination to project the kind of by-product tables, charts, articles, and reports that might be generated as a result.

I would also venture to predict that before the start of the twenty-first century, a giant stride further will be taken. Companies will be required to prepare annual Socio-Economic operating budgets. These would project in hard, practical dollar-supported terms what the organization expects to contribute to society in the forthcoming year.

# 7
# SOCIO-ECONOMIC OPERATING STATEMENT— THE FLAK

Socio-economic progress in America is being stymied by the "Yes, but——" approach.

Scores of businessmen, government officials, academicians, consumerists, and social scientists concede the need for social measurement and reporting designed to improve the corporate conscience. Then after confirming the need, they follow through with a stockpile of ifs, ands, and provisos. The upshot is that any attempts at positive action get suffocated by the rhetoric over methods and means.

The truth is that I know of no social measurement and reporting system proposed to date, or that might be developed in the future—including SEOS—that could not be whipped to the ground by a flock of objections and doubts.

Social action is tough to define, even harder to measure. Standard business functions can be complex, social functions more so. Keeping the public good in mind, it's not easy at this time for a corporation to accurately assess which programs it should launch and which it should halt.

But the task is less formidable than it appears at first, if we keep our basic goals in mind: to establish published social data that will provide corporate social action creditable visibility, as well as provide company-by-company comparisons within each industry.

By what steps can we reach this objective?

The problem lies not in the methodology, but in uniting the methodologists. Talk with a hundred professionals about social measurement and reporting. You'll get ten different action proposals and ninety different reasons to defer any move. I have examined several action recommendations proposed by men of good will. Most of them have merit. Some foster the SEOS concept in total or part. But rarely is the verdict "Go!" More often it boils down to "Yes, but——."

What does this indicate? Simply that a diversity of roads all lead in the same general direction—toward eventual formulation of the social measurement and reporting system we agree is so urgently needed. It's my view that the specific road traveled—so long as its feasibility can be supported—is less important than setting out on the journey.

SEOS has strong points in its favor. It is simple and inexpensive to achieve. It is easy to understand by all interested parties, businessmen and nonbusinessmen alike. It is the quickest and most effective way I know of today to get from Point A—no public visibility of corporate social actions—to Point B, visibility within each industry.

In attempting to achieve social measurement and reporting, we could computerize to the hilt. We could apply supersophisticated techniques that only a handful of scientists would comprehend. But in my view we already have overcomplicated the issue. Further complication would only deepen the muddle that currently exists and add a burdensome cost to the confusion.

SEOS will work well if we want it to work. But I have no intention of brushing aside the reservations and objections of men of good will. It is my conviction that most of the so-called roadblocks will dissolve themselves out of existence as SEOS gets under way and the state of the art is developed. Nonetheless, I shall attempt to analyze the major reservations concerning social reporting that have been called to my attention.

## The Artillery Barrage

### BIG GUN NO. 1

• *According to consumerists and business critics, an awe-some array of corporate social actions should be taken that aren't being taken. According to pragmatic managers concerned about company growth and survival, if some of the demands were complied with it would all but bankrupt the company. How does one draw the line between social responsibility and corporate irresponsibility?*

*Example:* A production process of XYZ Manufacturing Company is polluting a nearby river. Company engineers and consultants, after extensive study and investigation, conclude the degree of pollution and fish life jeopardy is minimal and well within Environmental Protection Administration constraints. Sportsmen and conservationists in the area disagree. They demand zero pollution, which they claim could be achieved through installation of a special filtering system. XYZ, having checked out the system, decides it is too costly for a company of its size. If the system were installed, in management's opinion the expenditure would seriously undermine XYZ's financial structure. But if conservationist demands are rejected, the president feels, it would mean a bad press. He believes the image would be smeared even more if exposed to public scrutiny via a Socio-Economic Operating Statement.

*Response:* The president's fears are unjustified. It is not a SEOS objective to pressure or force management into unreasonable social actions. In determining which programs to launch and which to discontinue, the company's interdisciplinary team would apply the "prudent man" principle of evaluation long used in the courts and in business decision-making.

To state the matter simply, in responding to social needs and demands, a businessman would be expected to do what a reasonable, prudent, and socially concerned executive might ordinarily do. No more, no less. The outside inter-disciplinary committee would in turn apply the "prudent man" rule in objectively auditing the corporate social actions and omissions reported by the internal team.

Inevitably, the selection of social improvements and detriments to include in the SEOS would become less of a problem as experience is gained. Industry practice would be established through usage. Professional associations and other groups would help to set guidelines. In borderline situations, outside consultants might be called in to offer impartial and objective judgments. As corporate social disclosure expands throughout industry, precedents will be set. In time today's harrowing decisions will become tomorrow's routine actions.

### CONFRONTING THE ISSUE

At the outset, however, the problem exists.

Before any company can bring social measurement and reporting to life, it must pose certain questions and evaluate the answers. Here is how one courageous organization faced up to the issue. Of particular attention to the late Eli Goldston, then president of Boston's Eastern Gas and Fuel Associates, were the following two questions:

• What are some internal (social) topics on which management can presently assemble and organize reasonably accurate and coherent data?

• Which issues of social accountability are of external interest, and to what extent are shareholders in particular interested, if at all?

In an attempt to get readings, the company included in its 1972 Annual Report a special information report and questionnaire directed to shareholders. In an open letter to shareholders, Mr. Goldston explained, "Many of our political, economic and commercial measures of progress have become obsolescent. We need a new kind of social accounting that goes beyond GNP for the nation and goes beyond net profits for the firm." He went on further to say that "many proposed imprecise measures of social accounting can be sufficiently accurate to be instructive. They are not hopelessly less accurate than GNP or net profit, and so they can be quite useful, even though they lack precision, for many purposes for which we cannot use GNP and net profit."

Four major areas of social concern were spelled out in the report, company actions and commitments made clear. These were industrial safety, minority employment, charitable giving, and pensions.

A questionnaire followed the report, with shareholder response and general comments invited. Designed as a detachable form, it folded into a self-addressed postage-free mailer. Completed questionnaires were tabulated and reviewed, response fed back to the shareholders.

Replies were instructive. They informed the company that:

• A large majority of shareholders approved such reporting.

• Shareholders welcome social information most of all on industrial safety, pensions, environment, and charitable giving. Slightly less interest was expressed in minority employment and consumer rights, much less in female employment by the predominantly male respondents.

• Sixty-one percent of shareholders rated the company good or fair on industrial accidents; 28 percent felt it was mediocre or poor.

• About 70 percent of shareholders felt the company should "move ahead of legal enforcement pressures" in the employment, promotion, and training of minorities; 57 percent opposed preferential hiring of minorities.

• Seventy-one percent believed Eastern should continue its present 1 percent level of charitable contributions. About 12 percent favored substantially increased donations; 14 percent felt the company should give nothing.

• Opinion was fairly well split with regard to types of charities: local, self-serving, social welfare, minority, etc.

• Sixty-seven percent favored the company's "matching gifts" program as a way of encouraging employee charitable contributions.

• A large majority of shareholders (85 percent of whom range in age from thirty-five to sixty-plus) favor more complete pension funding, vesting, portability, and inflationary adjustments for retired employees.

All of which proves that the information is there if one takes the time and effort to collect it. Needless to say, the shareholder is only one major source of social data. Others stem from the community, legislators, special groups, and the press. And however incomplete this may seem, it's a brave and practical start. Mr. Goldston's actions merited kudos for his imagination and initiative.

BIG GUN NO. 2

• *Is it realistic to expect a business enterprise to identify and report social detriments? Wouldn't corporate executives resist disclosures that might hurt the company image?*

*Example:* A midwest bank recently turned its back on community pressures to launch a minority hiring and training program. Its reason was that three months before it had installed a complex new computer system which was not running as anticipated. The result was serious communications problems, reduced worker morale, excessive absenteeism, a high rate of employee turnover. According to executive calculations it would be six months or more before the institution reverted to normal. It was certainly no time to initiate a major personnel program, however beneficial, that could only serve to complicate an already disrupted work environment. Bank officials explained this rationale to the press and minority group representatives. Minority people in particular, having had their fill of alibis and half-truths, took a dim view of the bank's explanation. Agitation multiplied, near-violence erupted. It triggered the worst press imaginable.

*Response:*Executive concern over negative revelations? It's an old story. Some managers lost sleep over SEC disclosure requirements four decades ago. The worry lines smoothed quickly enough when it became clear that honest disclosure—applicable to the competition, too—provided more benefits than hurts to the honorable businessman.

At first one might think that perhaps many managers' natural reactions to negative self-exposure would be to resist it. But after pondering realities, the thoughtful businessman would likely take a wholesome approach. First, negative self-exposure is not new to business. For decades companies have been making adverse financial conditions visible when they report contingent liabilities and set up reserves for litigation, bad debts, and the like.

The harsh reality is that we're in an era when disclosure, welcome or not, is a fact we'll have to live with. Increasing numbers of consumer and government groups are diligently monitoring corporate social performance. These groups report what they find or assume that they've found, sometimes from prejudiced points of view and in terms designed to serve their ends most effectively.

It is no news to anyone that often management motivations as reported by reformer extremists and corporate gadflies are in violent conflict with motivations as represented by company executives. Nor does it take unique talents to appreciate that since visibility will be given social detriments, like it or not, fair and objective exposure would be much to the advantage of the well-intentioned businessman.

The bank situation cited supports this contention. In cases of this kind, what makes news from the journalist's point of view? The bank official's logical, well-reasoned arguments for deferring the social program might make column 5 on page 38. But the fire and fury, the inflammatory statements, emotion-filled threats, and invective—or worse—would get page 1 billing.

In this case, let us assume bank management's position to be honest and valid. The bank's failure to launch the social program would not appear as a detriment on the Socio-Economic Operating Statement since a "prudent and reasonable" manager would not be expected to advocate such action at this time. The prevailing circumstances along with the bank's position—and concern—might simply appear in narrative form in the "Notes" section of the report.

BIG GUN NO. 3

• *Won't it take years to develop all the standards, indicators, and rules that will be needed to make SEOS an actuality?*

*Example:* In 1970, as consumers developed greater interest in nutrition, Del Monte Corporation created wall charts and cards that explain the Basic Four Food Groups, a simple guide to good nutrition. The materials were printed in English and Spanish. More than 1.2 million were distributed to schools, health departments, universities, and other groups. Mrs. Virginia Knauer, who was director of the White House Consumer Affairs Office, endorsed the educational effort. About 220,000 of the Spanish language materials were distributed in the United States, Puerto Rico, and Trinidad.[1]

*Response:* This voluntary program was of clear social value. Equally clear is the advertising and promotional value involved. The charts and other material gave positive exposure to the company's name and products. The question arises: In what measure was this a marketing or for-profit program, to what degree a "social improvement"? How does one properly allocate executive and other salaries, materials, production, and distribution costs relating to the program. Don't we need specific guidelines and rules to make a meaningful assessment and reporting?

*My answer:* If we wait for all the guidelines and rules that might be formulated to cover thousands of diverse situations and actions, it would be like waiting for all the nation's economists to agree on the guidelines and rules governing our economic existence. Intelligent observers will concede that our great, great grandchildren will never see this day.

We're again faced with the choice of simplifying the issue or complicating it beyond practicality. I have no wish to understate the importance of strong guidelines and rules. The point I want to make is that they need not be spelled out from A to Z at the outset.

We already have a multiplicity of standards and measures in social areas ranging from health and education to the environment and safety. Scientists know how to identify acceptable levels of noise and pollution. We have dependable measure of health and nutrition, tests to gauge literacy, or if a person is productively employable. Hard program inputs—the manpower, production, material, and overhead costs of social programs—are even easier to determine.

Our objective is a social measurement tool to give visibility and to make company-by-company comparisons within each industry. So long as apples and oranges in Company A are weighted fairly against apples and oranges in Company B, our purpose will be served. It would be obviously self-defeating to go through sophisticated computrobatics with the end goal in mind of apportioning 54.625 percent of the Del Monte consumer education program cost to "social improvement" and 43.375 percent to the marketing effort. It would serve our comparison tool objective far better, particularly at the outset, to simply represent known cost factors as fairly as possible.

What about potential revenues attributable to the program? I see nothing gained in attempting to subtract real or projected profits from social contributions. Financial gains make social improvements none the less beneficial. The ultimate rules and guidelines we seek will be developed through a combination of usage and research. The research, by government agencies, universities, industry associations, and private research groups, is already well on its way.

A treasure trove of indicator and guideline material

appeared in *Toward a Social Report,* the widely praised book published in 1969 by the Department of Health, Education, and Welfare. Since 1970, the Office of Management and Budget has been embarked on an ambitious program of structuring a set of national social indicators. Areas covered include health, public safety, education, employment, income, housing, leisure and recreation, and population. "Social concerns" are identical in each area. National totals are developed and broken down into components by age, sex, race, income, location, and other factors.[2]

Pioneering research has also been done by such groups as the National Science Foundation, the Organization for Economic Cooperation and Development in Paris, and the United Nations Statistical Office. The American Institute of Certified Public Accountants has formed a committee on social measurement which has been hard at work.

I have every confidence that from all of this effort will emerge a set of generally accepted practices such as we have seen in conventional accounting, law, and other professions. The key word is "emerge." It would be folly to think we could have the end product to start with.

BIG GUN NO. 4

• *You can't always put a dollar price tag on social action.*
*Example:* The United States Gypsum Company's land reclamation efforts consist of a variety of programs, according to information furnished Senator Frank E. Moss by the company's chairman, Graham J. Morgan. The report points out that only four states in which the company operates have legislation pertaining to the reclamation of land disturbed by open-pit mining or quarrying. Yet division works managers are advised to develop reclamation plans, whether required by law or not.

The report states further that A. P. Green Refractories, a USG subsidiary, turned an empty clay pit into a small lake with sanded shorelines. Employees at the company's Alabaster, Michigan, plant transformed a spoil-pile area into a nine-hole golf course. In Greenville, Mississippi, a USG reforestation program is reversing the side effects of a control flooding program that destroyed the natural growth pattern of cottonwood timber. The resource rehabilitation program, unique in the wood industry, call for 1,250 acres to be planted annually over twenty-five years.

*Response:* The programs referred to above are clearly socially productive. But how do you show the dollar investment on the Socio-Economic Operating Statement?

Illustration one, an ugly clay pit is transformed into an attractive scenic lake. Illustration two, a golf course is built to replace a blighted area. No price tag problem here. The cost of labor and materials can be spelled out easily enough as they would be in costing out any business operation. On the surface, at least, these appear to be purely social actions, the main motivation to eliminate scenic eyesores.

Assuming that the reclamation was undertaken voluntarily, the total cost of each project would appear as an improvement on the SEOS. With reclamation legally mandated, it would be a different situation. Even then some credit might be due. The question: Did creation of the golf course or lake exceed the company's legal requirements? If the company spent $25,000 to develop the land and shore area when it might have gotten by with a simple landfill operation for $10,000, the voluntary part of the investment would be $15,000, and that's the amount that would be reported.

The reforestation program, although socially beneficial, might be another matter entirely. The question here: Was it a business or socially motivated action? If it was a move a practical manager might be reasonably expected to make to ensure the future growth and well-being of his company, the social gain would be a by-product of the normal business action. This is precisely what happens when a socially beneficial product such as an effective new drug is introduced to the market. Since the company is in the drug business, the fruits of its profit-geared activity do not properly rank as voluntary social contributions.

No mining or woodlands expert, I'm not qualified to

judge the items cited above. But I believe the company's internal SEOS team, had one been formed, would be sufficiently knowledgeable to be able to differentiate between social and business investments, as would the external group of experts selected to audit the report.

In the large majority of social actions, a price tag isn't difficult to come by if blue sky factors and iffy projections are ruled out, and if ramifications that don't bear on hard money outlays are eliminated from the SEOS reporting. A classic example is the bank student loan program where applicants borrow at a reduced rate and receive easy repayment terms. Pricing out such a program could be brutally complex if we permit ourselves to get carried away by all the ramifications and projections involved.

Bernard L. Butcher, assistant to the executive vice president of the Bank of America, provides insight into what some of these factors might be: (1) future profits the bank might expect from new customers developed by the student loan program; (2) the bank's share of payout attributable to the increased income level of students who presumably would not have attended college without the loan; (3) increased bank business resulting from the increment to the area's economy because of the improved educational level generated.[3]

This is only a small sampling of the possible factors one might build into a program of this kind. I agree that attempting to include such items in the SEOS report would make the statement formidable to create.

The alternative road is simpler and less costly to travel. It is a straight calculation of the difference between bank income received from student loans and income that might have been expected were the funds channeled down conventional routes.

I have no quarrel with extensive analysis a company might wish to undertake before launching an ambitious social program. The nature and size of the investment would certainly govern the degree of consideration it merits. But for SEOS purposes, abstruse factors and hypotheses serve only to cloud the issue and make company comparisons difficult. It's unlikely that two large banks, each attempting to report all possible elements relating to a student loan program, would apply all of the same assumptions and conclusions in their reckoning.

Oliver Wendell Holmes once counseled: "We need elucidation of the obvious a good deal more than investigation of the obscure."

Social reporting critics tend to focus on the obscure; proponents stress the obvious. In the long run we will find that the simpler the approach, the easier the dollar sign tagging, the more meaningful the comparison structure.

### AND THOSE PESKY SMALL GUNS

• *The Socio-Economic Operating Statement's preparation will be too costly. It will mean adding several accountants to the staff.*

Nonsense! The same arguments echoed when pension funds were first proposed, the forty-hour week introduced, employee insurance benefits initiated. "The costs are prohibitive; they will drive us out of business."

We experience hundreds of business failures each year. I have yet to see one triggered by pension funds, the forty-hour week, or employee insurance benefits. Costs applicable to all companies within an industry become absorbed into the normal business operation. It happened when working hours were reduced from sixty to fifty to forty. It happened when social security was introduced. It happened when expanded disclosure was first required by new accounting and SEC rules.

Social reports prepared once or twice a year will be relatively inexpensive to produce. Offsetting the costs, a host of benefits will accrue, not only to society but to business as well. Not the least of these will be the accurate reading most companies will get for the first time with regard to their

*133*

social responsibilities and how they are being met as compared with competitors.

• *As increased social legislation is enacted, the need for social reports will diminish.*

Not so. We're living in dynamic times unprecedented in history. There's no telling from year to year what new problems and issues will erupt. One of today's chief concerns is with air and water pollution. One of tomorrow's main issues, only occasionally mentioned today, may well be sound pollution. Also virtually certain to take on added importance as waste continues to suffocate resources, the proliferation of products that are useless to society and serve to clutter the environment.

Nor are human expectations on the verge of declining. As the Institute for the Future points out in a Delphi forecast sponsored by four major U.S. companies, ". . . though America's economic standard of living will continue to climb, expectations of citizens will outrun the economy's ability to fulfill them."

I can visualize no curtailment of reportable social improvements and detriments in the foreseeable future.

• *Under SEOS, an improvement isn't credited if it's required by law. If the law calls for a specific social action, and the investment is deferred, it's reported as a detriment. But legislation in certain areas is sometimes unclear. Who qualifies as ultimate arbiter when management disagrees with social advocates over interpretation of the law?*

Safety is a good case in point. The Occupational Safety and Health Act, which became federal law in April 1971, lists over twenty-two thousand safety standards to be met by various industries. Over four million companies with fifty-seven million employees are subject to its provisions. Even businessmen concede that a tough safety law was long overdue. But safety officials have been swamped with complaints about OSHA's complexity. A National Small Business Association spokesman notes it would cost a firm $300 simply to buy all the literature needed to analyze the standards. Westinghouse Electric Corporation, for one, has set up a whole operation to interpret the act and disseminate information regarding it.

Now consider the plight of Kingpin Manufacturing Company. On the heels of a plant accident, the union has demanded that the company junk a $50,000 processing machine. If the more current model with special guards attached had been in operation, the union claims, the worker would not have been hurt. After studying the situation, management counters that the machine is safe; if the worker exercised normal and reasonable caution he would not have been hurt.

On whose side is the right? I'm not qualified to say. But again, experts in the field—within the company and the external audit group—would be competent to make fair judgments in such matters. In this case, the solution might be compromise, special guards designed for the existing machine. If the company failed to make this "prudent and reasonable" investment, it might be assessed as a detriment.

It's impossible to generalize regarding specific areas of social responsibility. Each case must be judged on its own merit. Sufficient expertise is available in every field to produce objectively fair and honest rulings.

Perfect rulings? That would be too much to hope for. As Norman Cousins once wrote, "The essence of man is imperfection. To talk about the need for perfection in man is to talk about the need for another species."

We find wide disagreement in our society with regard to court rulings. This doesn't cancel our need for the bench.

As human beings, we do the best we can. Because isolated problems are difficult to analyze and solve is no reason to discourage the social measurement and reporting system we so urgently need.

## Congressional Action

I see the Socio-Economic Operating Statement as a crucial first step in quantitatively assessing the corporate conscience. Critics may debate the format or labels. This is not significant. Refinements and modifications, always welcome when a new concept is launched, will inevitably upgrade both the exhibits and methodology as experience is gained.

Others will say it's okay to report voluntary dollar social program inputs, but what about the *quality* of outputs? This is at least equally important, and it's missing from SEOS. True. But it is vital to get started. And for a national movement of this scope and importance to get off the ground, it must be simple enough to apply on a wide-ranging basis without getting hopelessly tangled in undergrowth. It must be conceptually clear enough for all participants and evaluators to understand and apply in a standardized manner within each industry. It must be economically feasible for adoption by all business enterprises, prosperous or not. SEOS fulfills all these requirements.

Realistically, when we boil down the corporate conscience, what do you get? A consensus of individual consciences. Often this is dominated by the philosophy of one corporate leader.

Take John X, chairman and chief executive of X Products, Inc. Project into the future. It is SEOS time throughout his industry. Together with top aides, Mr. X reviews his company's Socio-Economic Operating Statement and compares it against the reports of his main competitors. Observing that X Products, Inc.'s, social contributions lag noticeably behind most of the competition's, his conscience is stirred. In his company as in most companies, a number of social-action decisions are hanging fire. Influenced at least in part by the SEOS comparative evaluations, Mr. X recommends moving ahead with certain actions that were too long deferred.

Now let's turn our camera on John Y, chairman and chief executive of Y Products, Inc. He, too, observes that his company's social contributions have been lagging behind the rest of the industry. But Mr. Y's single-track mind has been trained to focus exclusively on the bottom line of the profit and loss statement. He views his company's SEOS report with something less than enthusiasm. Let critics beef, he reasons. Let consumer advocates howl. If competitors want to go wild on social programs, let them. He's willing to sit back and enjoy any competitive advantage that may accrue as a result.

In my opinion, executives of Mr. X's attitude comprise the large majority of businessmen in our nation. Most executives are caring, conscionable, socially aware individuals. And most are realistic enough to appreciate that business has as much of a stake in America's social well-being as other factions of society.

Does this mean we should casually dismiss the minority of Mr. Ys? Not at all. I think controlling mechanisms can be established to make it less attractive for them not to carry their share of responsibility.

One such control would be congressionally enacted social incentives. Congress should enact legislation allowing companies a deduction against taxable income for net social expenditures shown on the social statement for the year that exceed a certain percentage of the taxpayer's net worth. I would recommend that such net socio-economic expenditures which exceed 1 percent of the net worth of a company be allowed as a full deduction from taxable income. This would be in addition to all other expense and depreciation allowances already made for these same items. Such a tax allowance would consciously assert the collective responsibility for our environmental and social problems by having government and the citizen-consumer indirectly share in the costs.

This special tax consideration would also help the socially conscientious manager to reap some fiscal rewards while pursuing his social action programs. It would help further to counter the "profits alone" arguments of the blinder-wearing businessman who refuses to look past the current profit and loss statement at the world beyond.

# 8

# THE
# INTERNAL/EXTERNAL
# HASSLE

At a recent symposium on corporate social responsibility two high-level executives engaged in debate.

One argued, "For social reporting to be meaningful, it must be prepared by an outside team of experts. Internal reports are bound to be prejudiced, to lack credibility, wind up as nothing more than high-sounding PR pronouncements."

His opponent disagreed. "What you propose is impractical and unrealistic. No outsider could understand the complex factors involved in attempting to pass judgment and report on the corporate conscience. He'd be unable to respond intelligently to the delicate balance that exists between a company's obligations to society and its stockholders."

The dispute is not uncommon. In my view, both arguments possess some validity.

Exclusively internal social measurement and reporting couldn't help but create the credibility gap referred to by debater number one. The public would have no reason to believe that an objective appraisal had been made.

Equally harrowing problems would be created if an outside group, however competent, were brought in to prepare the report. It would probably run into trouble accumulating all the information it would need for proper assessment and reporting. It would have difficulty understanding the impacts of certain corporate actions and decisions on society. It would experience problems attempting to weigh pressures from within against pressures from outside.

A practical way to deal with the internal/external hassle is to produce the Socio-Economic Operating Statement or its equivalent on an internal/external basis. This means having the report prepared in-house and audited by an outside team of experts.

## Pinpoint the Purpose

Step one in setting up a social reporting program is to clarify in your mind why you are doing it.

Basically, the report should fulfill four prime objectives:
• To help ensure the survival and well-being of free enterprise in general and the corporation in particular.
• To help cure the nagging ills of society.
• To respond conscientiously to pressures brought to bear by activist groups, the press and community, employees, investors, and government officials.
• To sustain the corporate conscience at a high level of morality and foster managerial pride in corporate actions and motivations.

The case for the purely private audit designed for inside distribution exclusively? I find it a hard one to make in face of the objectives set forth. A few feeble arguments emerge.

*A published social report could divulge confidential information.*

I see no reason why this should occur. Applying guidelines of "prudence" and "reasonableness," no company should feel obligated to reveal data detrimental to its earnings objectives.

*It would bring negative factors to the attention of activist groups and legislators which could result in unfavorable publicity or harassment.*

Corporate social responsiveness is being monitored more closely than ever before and this trend is on the upswing.

139

Experience proves repercussions from voluntary disclosure to be far less damaging than from disclosure by watchdog groups. What's more, what applies to one company in an industry would apply to all companies. The only firm that could suffer a competitive disadvantage would be the responsibility shirker.

*We'd need more extensive experience before making reports public.*

Evidence shows that the handful of companies already publicizing their social efforts—despite all the experimentation, failures, and bungling—have had their profiles upgraded as a result.

*Social involvement is purely a private matter, the corporation's own business and nobody else's.*

Sheer fantasy. The actions and attitudes of the corporation are so closely and complexly intertwined with the actions and attitudes of society that the public's right to be informed has been firmly established.


## The Selling Job

"It's one thing to satisfy the conscience pull from within," a public utility executive told me recently, "quite another to respond to the pressures from without. The first entails decisions tempered by morality and prudence. The second, in part at least, is a pure selling job. You have to respond conscionably on the one hand, and on the other convince people that you're doing it."

The social report would function as a powerful persuader. Urgent human needs have gone begging a long time in America. Endless studies have been made. Endless promises have been issued. Endless programs have been tried and endless failures chalked up. It's small wonder that cynicism cuts so deeply, that desperation runs high among the deprived, that confidence in business, in politics, in the American way of life stands at a low point in history.

At the same time—stirred by activist groups and the

media and fueled by early glimpses into the potentials of victim-organized power—expectations have never been higher. The explosion's inevitable.

"Pragmatically," my utility friend concedes, "the major concern plaguing us daily is to keep our constituent population of tigers off our back. The only way we can do this is to respond honestly and imaginatively to the human needs confronting us on a demand-priority basis and to simultaneously sell the public, investors, and our own people that the job we're doing is reasonable and fair."

Before management can hope to match actions to expectations, it must first pinpoint what the expectations are. One multiplant consumer products company recently launched a comprehensive, well-formulated program to target in on community needs on the one hand and upgrade its own credibility on the other.

An internal committee was organized to identify the corporation's most pressing social obligations and priorities. In time a formalized social report will outline actions taken in response to these needs. Included on the committee are some directors who represent outside points of view: a law professor for one, an economist–sociologist for another. These men's perspectives will be helpful in maintaining the internal/external balance. At the same time, their presence will add credibility to the effort.

Although there's no way of telling for sure, in the past this company appears to have been more conscionable than the average in its social responsiveness. Yet in recent years it has borne the brunt of rather vehement attack from student, consumer, and other activist groups.

"We were probably asking for it," the company's chairman admits. "If we learned one thing it's that you can't cast social investment seeds mindlessly about in the hope they'll take root in fertile soil. Social involvement warrants the same kind of reasoned and intelligent evaluation a business would apply to its profit-directed investments."

Today the committee is in the process of polling activist groups and other interested factions outside the company.

It sends questionnaires to student and faculty organizations, sounds the thinking of investors and government officials.

"The ideal," notes a spokesman, "is to pinpoint needs as they really exist, not as interpreted by the chief executive or a principal shareholder."

Off the record, he adds, "I can recall from the old days more than one occasion when corporate response to social obligations centered primarily around a financial contribution to one individual's favorite charity or to the political party of his choice. Them days are gone forever."

## *Top Down Approach*

If corporate responsibility is to work, it must start at the top and work its way down. Some signs are encouraging. Studies show that over 90 percent of the largest U.S. corporations already have assigned formal responsibility to monitor and report on the corporate conscience to high-level executives or committees.

New York's Chase Manhattan Bank is a typical example. There a consultant was hired to form a top-level social audit group. Having identified individual priorities, among other activities, Chase now conducts special loan and other economic programs to help revive stagnant urban areas. At Atlantic Richfield Company a high-level Public Affairs Committee reviews broad, conceptual proposals for new social responsibility projects. Equitable Life Assurance Society's president J. Henry Smith personally pinpoints senior vice presidents to take over specific social responsibility programs.

The top down trend is accelerating. But before constructive action can result, it's essential that top management be kept well abreast of the state of the conscience as it currently prevails.

Realistically, the typical chief executive is confused by what's happening. Attacked by the growing rhetoric and countervailing pressures from many directions at once, he's not certain what or whom to believe. Distrustful of self-appointed critics, he's at a loss to sort the valid social needs from the preposterous demands. The conclusion is clear. He needs to be informed.

The overriding objective is for the top executive to be able to answer to his personal satisfaction that the company is doing all that can be reasonably expected. He needs the input to respond for two main reasons: first, to justify his company's behavior in terms of his own self-image; second, to be able to defend his company's responsiveness to the critics lined up at his door.

A head of an industrial products company I know can attest to this need from personal experience. On a day he'd like to forget he drew flak from an emotional but articulate gadfly at the company's annual meeting. Involved was a sensitive social issue. After the meeting, still somewhat shaken, he was attacked by the press.

"I didn't make a *complete* fool of myself," he confided, "but I was frankly embarrassed. I was also acutely aware I had been inadequately prepared to respond to my assailants."

He's resolved never to get into a similar bind again. Next day he brought top aides together and began laying out a program. In hard, specific terms he set down his determination.

"I want to know what the law requires us to do," he said. "I want to know what we *are* doing and why. I want to know what we are failing to do and why. I want to know what others in the industry are doing and what it is costing them to do it."

The machinery has now been set in motion to provide this information. Needless to say, if companies within each industry had been producing the proposed Socio-Economic Operating Statement on a periodic basis, my friend would not have had to search for the information he required.

A chief executive should also be able to gauge with some accuracy the degree of social responsiveness that will satisfy the community on one balance of the scale, stockholders on the other. This problem will pretty much solve itself in time as a growing number of companies produce social reports; reporting formats become formalized and familiar; developmental efforts by industry associations, universities and foundations, the accounting profession, and others begin to pay off.

Meanwhile community needs, real and perceived or both, may take some hard work to pinpoint. There will be a continuing need to take the social pulse periodically. A movement in this direction is already underway with several companies polling the communities in which they operate. First National Bank of Minneapolis is a good example. In its probe of community needs it has identified ten quality-of-life factors that apply to the Twin Cities. These include among others job opportunities, transportation, and health. The bank is now developing measures for each factor that will enable it to channel its resources with maximum effectiveness.

After surveying the community, the trick is to weed out from the multiplicity of needs that exist the appropriate areas of involvement. A practical way to do this, notes McKinsey & Company consultant Terry McAdams, is to review performance across all social categories and identify areas of high vulnerability or opportunity. He offers this brief questionnaire as a guide.

• Is anyone's life, health, or safety endangered by our actions or product?

• Do we comply with all laws and regulations—federal, state, and local?

• What are the major in-house concerns regarding our social responsibility performance?

• What will be the impact of continuing a given activity—on our employees, customers, stockholders, and the public in general?

• If we change our actions will our constituencies understand why? Will they misinterpret our motives?

• Is new legislation likely to be implemented which will regulate this activity?

- What action has our competition taken? Industry in general?
- Can we estimate the total cost of each activity area?[1]

Respond to these questions, McAdams suggests. You should then be able to assess which activity areas are most vulnerable to criticism, which are most in need of improvement by increasing current efforts or implementing new ones, which present opportunities to help solve pressing social problems while expanding the business.

Finally, adds G. Robert Truex, executive vice president for social policy for the Bank of America, "How do we report to the president on [the bank's] performance in these mainstream areas?"

He suggests that, "at the end of each year, a performance report be prepared discussing as specifically as possible the following aspects of each key issue: First, the potential of that issue—either to affect the bank favorably or unfavorably. Second, the progress made in the previous year in dealing with the issue. Third, the bank's current position or standing on each issue. Fourth, the problems encountered."[2]

It is interesting to note that in the process of preparing and producing the Socio-Economic Operating Statement, each of these points would be resolved.

## Objectives in Conflict

It happened in a medium-sized New England manufacturing company. The president was a man of conscience, sensitive to society's needs and his own moral responsibilities. He had no way of comparing his company's social investment against the investment of competitors, but he instinctively felt it should be doing more.

Summoning his executive vice president, he conveyed his feelings. His aide agreed. The president already had done some preliminary investigation. He had spelled out three social-action priorities: increased minority hiring and training; elimination of a marginally safe product; installation of employee safety equipment in the plant.

"It's only a start," the president said, "but I think it should be made and made right away."

He delegated to the executive vice president the task of implementing the three social actions outlined. The manager's first move was to meet with the plant manager, marketing vice president, and personnel director. The personnel manager was all for minority hiring in whatever areas and to whatever extent the chief executive wished.

His superior instructed, "The boss wants more blacks and Puerto Ricans in the plant, office, and sales department. And he doesn't mean in low-rated jobs. He wants black supervisors and sales representatives."

The plant manager and marketing executive didn't openly object, but they reacted with tight-lipped resentment.

"Where are we going to find qualified people?" the marketing man wanted to know.

"Look hard enough and you'll find them," the executive vice president replied. He turned to the personnel man for confirmation.

"I'll do the best I can," he was told.

On the other two issues the executive vice president met open resistance, resistance he could understand and appreciate.

The plant manager protested, "The kind of safety equipment you're talking about would knock a mile wide hole in our earnings figures for the year."

The marketing manager was equally upset over the mandate to phase out a profitable product.

The executive vice president was embarrassed. He was torn on the one hand between his chief's instructions and his own stirrings of conscience and on the other by his commitment to profits. No one understood better than he the pressures these men were under from the board, the chief, himself, to improve earnings results. Their reputations, incomes, and growth with the company were all geared to performance. He could vividly recall numerous sessions where the screws were applied. How do you tell a man in the morning that he has to work like the devil to boost profits and in the afternoon make demands that in his view could defeat that objective?

Management professed to believe in a doctrine of relative autonomy and independence for its executives. This was just the reverse. The executive vice president tried to act tough, but he couldn't feel tough. He made high-sounding remarks about social responsibility which, like motherhood, no one could dispute. But what it boiled down to was a considerable capitulation.

"You know what the boss wants," he told the three managers. "Do it the best way you can and as fast as you can."

You probably can guess the result. Some token moves were made to adhere to the mandate. A few blacks were hired, one even given the title of "supervisor," though he performed no supervisory function. A few inexpensive safety gadgets were installed. Instead of chopping the unsafe product from the line, production was cut back slightly under the rationale that it would be gradually discontinued over a period of time.

In sum and substance the social actions taken cost the company a pittance and had little significance.

It's an oft-told tale, unfortunately. Executives often face a double-barreled dilemma. On the one side they're hemmed in by corporate pressures to boost earnings, cut costs, keep prices down, and on the other side by social demands. Not surprisingly, they're at a loss as to how to proceed.

The dilemma forms an inevitable conclusion. For corporate social investment to pay off and work, it must be planned and formulated with no less care than a marketing, research, or product development effort. An increasing number of managers are awakening to this reality. Notes John L. Paluszek, who heads Corporate Social Action, Inc., a management consulting firm that specializes in social responsibility, "We are now getting down to business in our handling of the corporate social responsibility function. Corporate philanthropy in its traditional form—charity without carefully thought out cost-benefit standards—is dead."[3]

Paluszek cites the approaches of some leading U.S. corporations.

Whirlpool Corporation, notes a spokesman, budgets for social activity "exactly the way we budget for other company functions . . . . Based on the experience we've had we can pretty well identify the projects we want to undertake, develop, or complete in the coming year. We identify the costs—in addition to our manpower—and we submit an itemized recommendation to the Whirlpool financial committee. However, the budget is a base guideline. If we come across an additional opportunity for achieving our objectives and can justify the expenditure, our management is generally ready to accept such a recommendation."

According to Levi Strauss & Company, effective corporate response to social problems "requires a pool of money that is predictable and not dependent on whim . . . . To this end, we have pledged a minimum of three percent of after-tax income." The pool, he adds, is in addition to normally related business expenses such as the cost of product integrity and equal opportunity hiring.

First Pennsylvania Bank frequently funds corporate responsibility programs out of corporate executive overhead. If the program succeeds and grows, it is absorbed into the operating structure, with costs shared by the departments involved.

Standard Oil of Indiana feels that "as difficult as it may be, attempts must be made to establish specific goals, quantify costs and benefits, fix responsibility, and set timetables for achievement." It contends that this approach is accepted procedure in the achievement of traditional corporate goals and that social goals will not achieve credibility, and be implemented, unless the same procedure is applied to them.

In short, budgeting for social improvement must be closely akin to budgeting for earnings improvement.

## *How Much?*

What size corporate social budget meets the standard of conscionable on the one tack, "prudent and reasonable" on the other?

A businessman I know applies his own self-devised guideline. When faced with hard budget allocation decisions on specific social actions, he asks himself the soul-searching question: "If the issue were exposed to tough public scrutiny, how would we fare?"

A conscience-prodded approach. But testy at best and weighted against the conscionable executive at worst. Yet where can this obviously concerned manager turn for real guidance?

Our current financial reporting system, sophisticomputerized to the hilt, sheds little if any light on social actions beneficial or adverse. It is thus essentially irrelevant where the evaluation of corporate social response is concerned.

What we need is as clear as it's urgent. Social and nonsocial activities must be kept separate and apart in both budgeting and reporting. Gradually but too slowly across the nation managers are awakening to this realization. A bank now keeps a separate record of expenses associated with its community relations programs. A packing company isolates projected expenditures for pollution control equipment in its capital budget. Others set up special funding for social activities and separate records to match.

However incomplete and fragmented such efforts are, at least they're a start in the right direction. But we need more than a start. We need a hard momentum-forcing shove.

The issue is too serious to disregard or delay. *The Wall Street Journal* frankly poses the question: "How can a profit-and-loss statement be made to reflect the good a company does by assigning some of its personnel to advising minority businessmen struggling to succeed in a ghetto?

*149*

How can the installation of pollution-control devices at a factory be shown at the bottom line as a positive accomplishment rather than a drain on productivity?"

It goes on to cite a prediction of what the ultimate answer will be. "D. S. Langsdorf, senior vice president and comptroller of the Bank of America, predicts that within three to five years annual reports will be required to include data on a company's social outlays. Some authorities foresee complete 'social audits' of firms by outside consultants within a decade, just as outside accountants conduct financial audits today. A biweekly newsletter that reports on corporate social involvement, predicts that eventually ratings of a company's 'social performance' will be as readily available as rating of its credit-worthiness."

When this inevitable day arrives, the problem of how much to budget for corporate social responsibility will pretty much be resolved.

## The PR Payoff

I know a businessman who is currently under siege by social activists in his community because of a stream temporarily discolored by a nontoxic plant effluent. Local residents contacted health authorities, environmental officials, conservationist groups, and the press. They swarmed down on the company like a horde of locusts. As a result, its image was seriously smeared.

My friend is exasperated. "It's unfair," he complained. "Last year my company invested a sum exceeding two percent of after-tax earnings on social programs and improvements. That's well above average and from what we can surmise more than any of our competitors. Yet for a relatively minor violation we get dragged through the mud as if we were the most antisocial organization in town. We enforce the highest product safety and quality standards in the industry. We're ahead of the time in such areas as equal opportunity and minority hiring. We spend thousands on

waste control facilities. We engage in all kinds of philan-
thropies. But except for our own PR releases, which are
taken with the proverbial grain of salt, news of our substantial and positive contributions receive scant if any
attention."

This manager has a point. But it's pointless to sound off
about inequities without facing the realities and doing
something about them. The communications gap is
apparent.

For all of the sophisticated economic and financial intelligence systems at work in society, we have no nationally
accepted vehicle for reporting the extent of a company's
social involvement. Nor do we have any nationally recognized third party arbiters to give credibility to corporate
social reports as with financial statements.

Many thoughtful businessmen are beginning to voice the
urgency of plugging this gap with a measurement, reporting, and auditing system that will help to set the record
straight. For the responsible businessman, it could be worth
several public relations departments.

My guess is that public ignorance regarding corporate
social involvement far surpasses public ignorance regarding
corporate profits. The analogy's a good one. Although the
"profit story" has received widespread publicity, the truth is
that the American people are woefully misinformed and far
off on the issue. According to a 1971 year-end survey of
1,000 adults and 479 teenagers, after-tax profits are esti-
mated at 28 cents on the sales dollar. The real figure is
closer to 4 cents.

This is the highest profit reading taken in such a poll over
a twenty-six–year period. "One reflection of widespread
economic ignorance," notes Princeton's Opinion Research
Corporation, which conducted the survey, "is the public's
belief that wage hikes can be financed out of existing
profits. Two-thirds of the American people believe that
most companies can afford to raise wages ten cents per hour
without raising prices. Only a fourth disagree."

Now contrast this with prevailing ignorance regarding

the extent of corporate social involvement and the degree of social investment most companies can afford. Random samplings indicate that a majority of citizens believe that the large corporations could easily cure half the ills of society if they only wanted to. If they did nothing else, periodically prepared and externally audited corporate social reports would help to dispel this notion and present the public with the facts.

They would also help businessmen in the sometimes ticklish task of attempting to pinpoint what the "public interest" really is.

One manager I know is presently in the throes of trying to decide whether adding a safety control to a mass-produced home appliance would be socially beneficial or not.

"The hazard," he claims, "is minimal. The unit has only rarely been known to fail. When it does only minor shock could result. No serious injury was ever reported. True, if we add the device it would eliminate even the remote possibility of failure. But it would boost the price of the work-saving product almost eight percent. Fewer people could afford it. So what's the socially beneficial action to take?"

Such borderline judgments are not uncommon with regard to products, projects, and programs.

Another company produces a mildly noxious gas in its manufacturing processes. Its best efforts to contain the vapor has resulted in less than 2 percent escaping into the environment. Again, the adverse effects are judged "minimal" by outside consultants. To contain the final 2 percent would cost twice the sum already invested to contain the 98 percent. It would also hike the price of the product to a point where it might become marginally marketable. Containment could thus jeopardize the whole operation, throw a few hundred people out of work. Equally true, the environment would be fractionally cleaner.

What price social benefit? It's hard to say at times.

Another question: Under what conditions is a manager expected to abandon a profitable product, opportunity, or objective for the "good of society"?

The "good of society" is not always easy to define. Sometimes what it boils down to is, who yells loudest.

There are no simple answers to such dilemmas. But a comprehensive system of social reporting would at least help sort the detriments and improvements. Business and its problems have a way of repeating, if not piece by piece, in sufficient general context to provide a bank of experience for management reference. As increasing numbers of social reports become available for comparison and analysis, the new breed of corporate social managers will become increasingly well equipped to arrive at judgments and decisions.

When it comes to wrestling with hard specific issues like those cited above, the body of professionals who serve as external social auditors will in time develop the kind of expertise required to assist in the decision-making process.


## Toward a Relevant Rhetoric

Many corporations still regard the new social pressures being exerted on them as more of a public relations problem than an investment decision. Not surprisingly, as demands multiplied during the first half of this decade, so did the rhetoric. Some recent top executive pronouncements:

". . . the future growth and success of this company rest on how well we meet the urgent needs of people."

". . . our intention is to function as a people-oriented company, first, last, and foremost."

". . . the good of society and the good of the corporation are one and the same; they interact interchangeably."

". . . the first responsibility of business is to operate for the well-being of society."

Scores of such statements could be listed. Some are sincere, others pure pap. The classic abuse, notes Joel F. Henning, was recently perpetrated by a large woodlands company. Its ad depicted an idyllic river scene with the caption, "It costs us a bundle, but the Clearwater River still runs clean." Henning notes, indeed it does, where the photo was taken, *upstream* of the company's pulp plant.

What companies say, he adds, is often more inspiring than what they do. He cites examples to support his contention.

"When Gordon Sherman, president of Midas-International, demonstrated a solid commitment to corporate responsibility with financial contributions to Saul Alinsky's activities and others like him, he was forced out of the company in a bitter proxy battle against the company's chairman, Nate H. Sherman, Gordon's father . . . .

"The insurance industry's much publicized two-billion dollar pledge for low income urban housing and related projects began with a bang in 1967 but is fizzling out. As the program ends, the balance of funds is going increasingly into commercial loans to business, not into housing . . . ."

When Honeywell Corporation's chairman was questioned about war contracts by shareholders, he defined corporate responsibility as "hiring a man to make speeches on free enterprise and against communism at local groups." One such employee, John Fergus, notes Henning, was convicted of conspiracy to libel former U.S. Senator Thomas Kuchel, a liberal.

"Even in the conventional and benign area of charitable contributions," Henning adds, "corporate performance is unimpressive. One study indicates that corporate charitable gifts go overwhelmingly to conservative and inoffensive organizations engaged in marginally productive welfare programs. And overall corporate beneficence is dwindling. In 1969 corporate charitable giving dropped below 1 percent of pretax profits, compared with 1.11 percent as recently as 1967. The bigger the corporation, the smaller the percentage of net income it gives away."[4]

Fortunately two teams man the rope in every tug of war. Gloomy tales abound, but there are hopeful signs too that many conscience—*and survival*—driven managers are working hard to give credence to the rhetoric of social responsibility with meaningful action. As we'll see in the next chapter, increasing numbers of U.S. corporations are endeavoring to meet their social obligations head-on with a lot more than talk.

Traditionally, a key communications center for lip service long has been and still is the annual report. In recent years, however, a new dimension of public service has been added to the self service. If anything the rhetoric has multiplied, which is to be expected in response to the pressures. But it seems to be changing as well.

States Battelle Memorial Institute's Meinolf Dierkes and Robert Coppock: "The amount of reporting of socially responsible actions steadily increased through all the years selected (1965 to 1971). To us, this clearly indicates that managers, especially in large companies, are increasingly becoming aware of the fact that the success of their enterprises depends upon the way in which they adjust to changes in society."

In their sampling of 285 big corporation annual reports, the writers document the number of "mentions" by subject: Environmental protection heads the list with 40 percent of the mentions; next with 26 percent is the general area of corporate philanthropy; 14 percent of the statements deal with general problems of social involvement without mentioning specific fields of concern or activity.

So much for the rhetoric. But what does it add up to? The main question as posed by Dierkes and Coppock is, "How serious are corporations' activities and their concern with social problems? Do they represent just verbal statements— public relations activities—or did the companies under study really take action in these fields?"

They follow through with the answer: "About half of the company reporting was made in relatively specific terms, which indicates that the growing attention companies are paying to the new dimensions of social expectations is a serious, nonsuperficial, concern. Perhaps most significant of all, note the pollsters, "Of all the statements concerning social responsibility, approximately 24 percent dealt with actions in progress and 50 percent with actions already completed. Variations among industries were not significant."[5]

155

So the wheels appear to be grinding, much too slowly of course, but grinding. It's still difficult at times to distinguish between the honest rhetoric and the self-serving palaver.

Which swings us back full circle to the social report. The Socio-Economic Operating Statement would in time serve to expose the purely gaseous rhetoric for the insubstantial vapor it is. It would reinforce the honest rhetoric with the concrete evidence of action and results. Finally, it would help to produce a relevant rhetoric of its own—an independent visibility vehicle for the conscience-driven manager and the company he represents.

# 9
# THE
# SNOWBALLING
# MOMENTUM

Justice Louis Brandeis noted almost sixty years ago: "Publicity is justly commended as a remedy for social and industrial diseases. Sunlight is said to be the best of disinfectants; electric light the most efficient policeman."

Encouragingly, more light is being shed these days on corporate social action and omissions than ever before, much of it by activist groups, much of it by corporate progressives.

One reason for the current publicity surge is the upgrading of executive consciences on many business fronts. Another is the growing sophistication of citizen groups that are honing watchdog techniques and effectively reporting what they monitor. A third is the increasing number of general and specialized publications giving added exposure to social issues in response to public demand.

Early in 1973, for example, *News Front* devoted a comprehensive special report to the spotlighting of U.S. corporate leaders in social responsibility. In a separate box it listed the "20 Top Performers" in alphabetical order. I think they are worth relisting here.

Abbott Labs
Alcoa
Bank of America
Dreyfus Third Century Fund
Eastman Kodak
Exxon
Firestone
First National Bank of Chicago
Ford
General Motors
IBEC
IBM
Levi Strauss
Olin
Spring Mills
U.S. Steel
Xerox
Advertising Council
National Association of Businessmen
World Press Institute

On an industry-by-industry basis, it highlighted specific social contributions of these and other leaders. It cited DuPont's 1972 contribution of $2,575,000 to teaching and research in 149 institutions; American Metal Climax's *Environmental Monthly* citation for pollution control at its Washington plant where particulate emissions were cut 97 percent; Owens Corning Fiberglas for its Jobs for Vets program with over 40 percent of manufacturing personnel hired in 1972 Vietnam veterans. It also noted Con Edison's rolling blood lab and clinic, testing for lead poisoning and sickle-cell anemia in New York City children; IBM's efforts in establishing plants in ghetto areas and making them work; Sperry & Hutchinson for hiring minority employees in at least equal proportion to the total population in the area; and a good deal more.

Companies too are telling the public more about the hard specifics of their social involvement. They're doing it in annual reports, special reports, and at shareholders meetings. A *Business Week* survey of one-hundred major corporations reveals that the percentage of companies reporting on corporate responsibility more than doubled from 30 percent in 1970 to 64 percent in 1972.

Candor lends credence to responsibility claims, the survey report points out. Executives increasingly recognize that candor means hard dollar evidence and not broad moralizing on the subject. It is significant, I think, that almost two-thirds of the reports in the *Business Week* sampling contain sections on pollution control, minority hiring practices, and general corporate citizenship.

Scovil Manufacturing Company's 1972 annual report as an example included a "Social Action Report" in the form of a balance sheet. Under the employment opportunities section, the company cites as an asset an increase in minority employment from 6 percent in 1963 to 19 percent the previous year. Balancing this in the liabilities column is the statement that the company needs "more upgrading of minority employees into higher grade jobs."

Except for past year performance figures, the entire content of First Pennsylvania Corporation's 1972 report consisted of interviews on social issues conducted by John R. Bunting, the company's chairman. Interviewees ranged from Ralph Nader and Carl B. Stokes, Cleveland's former mayor turned commentator, to White House assistant Barbara Hackman.

On a full page devoted to social responsibility, the Atlantic Richfield Company said it had removed one-thousand billboard signs in thirty-six states because "overcommunicating can be deleterious." It also promised to increase to $1 million its deposits in minority-owned banks. The Graniteville Company, a textile producer, featured a *male* model on its cover strutting down the runway, with women looking on.

First National Bank of Minneapolis devoted the major portion of its twenty-four–page annual report to social issues under such headings as "The annual social environmental audit . . . A problem and a proposal." Con Edison of New York's report contains sections devoted to the ecological and social environments with specific contributions in each spelled out.

Several companies have foundations set up with social responsibility as their major thrust. Cummins Engine Company, for example, contributes up to 5 percent of pretax profits to its separately incorporated foundation "mandated to affirm and promote humane living." The foundation's annual report lists scores of social programs, contributions, and grants with each item specified by recipient and dollar amount. Total disbursements for one recent year amounted to almost $1½ million. Dayton Hudson Corporation has a similar setup with foundation contributions listed as of fiscal year end January 31, 1972, at $2,259,191.

In addition to the annual reports published by corporations and their foundations, a rash of special reports devoted to social issues and the community are beginning to appear. CNA Financial Corporation, operating under the premise that "a corporation's prosperity depends on the health of the community in which it lives," puts out an annual social report titled *CNA and the Community*. Included is a three-page rundown of the company's "Grants and Contributions." Quaker Oats Company publishes a yearly "Social Progress Plan," laying out programs for the year ahead. Its table of contents lists such items as Food and Nutrition, Employment Opportunity, Environmental Quality, Consumerism, Minority Enterprise, Education, Drug Use and Abuse, Youth Programs, and Social Progress Budget which runs into several millions of dollars.

### Rhetoric and Then Some

Slowly but relentlessly the momentum is building. It is clear that a growing number of companies are putting their money where it counts.

To what extent is the rhetoric over social concern being backed by hard coin of the realm? In a preliminary effort to find out, a survey directed by John J. Corson was conducted under the auspices of the Committee for Economic Development. A questionnaire was sent to 800 large manufacturing, distribution, and service corporations. Of the 244 respondents, only 4.6 percent had a yearly sales volume under $99 million. Respondents worked from a comprehensive CED list of social programs that a business might pursue. These were outlined under the following headings: Economic Growth and Efficiency, Education, Employment and Training, Civil Rights and Equal Opportunity, Urban Renewal and Development, Pollution Abatement, Conservation and Recreation, Culture and the Arts, Medical Care, and Government.

Participants were asked whether they had, since January 1, 1972, attempted to inventory or assess their activities in these areas. The survey report notes that, "a surprising 76 percent said they had. Among those who had made an inventory or assessment, 88 percent said it covered more than one area on the list. The larger a company, the more likely it has made a social audit."

Respondents were also asked whether they felt that business firms in the future would be *required* to make social audits. Even at this early date, more than a third answered "Yes."

Significantly, they were questioned with regard to important obstacles they saw in the development of social audits. Two of these were judged most crucial by respondents: (1) inability to develop measures of performance that everyone will accept; (2) inability to make creditable cost/benefit analyses to guide company actions.

Lesser obstacles cited in order of importance are: inability to develop consensus as to what activities shall be covered; inability to develop consensus ways to organize information (more on this later in the chapter when I discuss the proposed formation of a Peace Production Board); dangers to the company in publishing the results of social audits; general decline in pressures on business to undertake social programs.

This last is rather surprising; and I suspect based on mis-

*161*

information, or ostrichization. It must be clear to most observers of the modern scene that pressure on corporations to address themselves to this nation's social problems have risen geometrically in recent years and today stand at an all-time peak. Regarding other obstacles listed, it is my conviction that a year or two after the widespread implementation of some kind of social measurement and reporting such as the SEOS, they will be deemed to be inconsequential.

## Pioneers of Social Progress

Inevitably, during any period of history when a trend toward social reform is experienced, a handful of imaginative leaders emerge to hack through the undergrowth to beat a path for others to follow. Henry Ford helped unshackle the "wage slave" when he cut the work day from nine hours to eight, introduced profit-sharing on a mass employee basis, and set the minimum wage at $5 a day. More recently, such innovators as Chrysler and Whirlpool pioneered in the upgrading of service by creating toll-free consumer "hot lines" which customers with problems and complaints can use to get prompt attention.

So has it been with all reform movements since the beginning of recorded history. The turbulent seventies are no exception. Again we see on the scene a comparative handful of major corporations, spurred most commonly by imaginative and conscionable chief executives who are well ahead of the pack.

The soul-searchings, sacrifices, and at times floundering experimentation are not to be underrated nor understated. Given the present state of the conscience-building art, the efforts sometimes serve to cloud the short-term profit picture. But it is characteristic of trail blazers to take the long-range view and remain mindful of the total picture. Armed with this perspective they know that over the long pull all of business will benefit from their endeavors, and their own organizations most of all.

Obviously there is not sufficient space in these pages for

acknowledgment of all important contributors and innovators in the field of social responsibility. Inevitably many
will be omitted due to oversight, space restrictions, because
the story wasn't disseminated, or because the program is
still too new for the story to be told. I'm sure some of the
contributions omitted are as significant as or more significant than some of those included. Thus what follows is but
a sampling of important corporate social innovations
reported to date.

I think I can safely predict that by 1978 a majority of the
nation's more important newspapers, magazines, and
radio–TV networks will periodically give public recognition
to corporations demonstrating leadership in their responsiveness to social issues. The trend is already under way.

POLAROID CORPORATION, one of the nation's earliest social
leaders, received a *Business Week* award in 1972 for innovations and contributions too numerous to outline in detail.
Among the highlights reported, some 12 percent of the
company's nearly ten thousand U.S. employees are black,
with 6.4 percent in salaried jobs. Another 3 percent are disadvantaged in other ways: physically or mentally handicapped, or with a poor grasp of English. A five-year-old
Polaroid subsidiary in Boston's black ghetto of Roxbury
continues to expand. There, 243 "unemployable" workers
have learned enough skills to graduate to regular jobs at
Polaroid and elsewhere. Polaroid is involved with 143 community projects in Greater Boston and New Bedford, Massachusetts, ranging from camera loans to family planning
services.

Particularly noteworthy is the company's deep involvement in the politically sensitive area of prison reform.
Behind its urging for other companies to employ ex-convicts, more than 150 have been hired by Polaroid during the
past several years, with only two returning to prison. In
Massachusetts the company is helping to rewrite archaic
laws and push them through the legislature. At least two
dozen Polaroid people have been drafted for projects
behind prison walls. The company's most conspicuous internal program is in education. Classes are conducted, often

163

on company time, on everything from basic English to advanced chemistry. The report notes that an astounding 20 percent of Polaroid's employees are in the educational curriculum.

OWENS-ILLINOIS, another award winner, enjoys the rather unique distinction of having been praised by no less a corporate critic than Ralph Nader. Nader cited Owens-Illinois as "one of the very few pulp and paper companies that has consistently made it a practice over the last twenty years to install the best pollution-control systems available—or to pioneer in developing new ones—almost always in advance of state requirements." The company has chalked up an outstanding record of environmental performance. Its paperboard mills, glass, and packaging materials facilities are ranked among the nation's cleanest. Owens-Illinois' late chairman R. H. Mulford set out the company's role in a policy memo which read in part: "We attach the same importance to air and water pollution abatement that we attach to quality, safety, fire prevention, and operating efficiencies."

Adhering rigidly to this credo, management has made imaginative innovations in pollution control. It was the first to install recovery boilers to capture spent cooking liquors, a major papermaking pollutant. It mapped out new methods to remove most of the sulfurous "rotten egg" odor from its mills. It also pioneered extensively in the recovery of chemicals and recycling of water to offset abatement costs. It is especially significant that Owens-Illinois is one of the very few companies that affirms that the 1972 Federal Water Pollution Control Act's goal of "zero discharge" by 1985 is not only achievable but "absolutely necessary."

LEVI STRAUSS & COMPANY's reputation is still hard to surpass. It routinely allocates 3 percent of net profits to a rash of community projects ranging from an intensive care unit for a Tennessee children's hospital to a program to get funding for Alabama's impoverished Green County. Levi Strauss plants were fully integrated long before the Equal Employment Opportunity Commission applied pressures toward this end. Its 33 percent minority employment statistic is impressive. Nearly 14 percent of the company's managers and officials were women in 1971, double the proportion of the previous year, 10.1 percent were classified as minority employees. In addition, the company buys massive supplies of goods and services from minority suppliers.

FAIRCHILD CAMERA & INSTRUMENT CORPORATION was given recognition, largely for its pioneering efforts at its semiconductor plant on the Navajo reservation at Shiprock, New Mexico. The small and troubled plant was conscientiously nursed by plant manager Paul W. Driscoll through the 1969–1970 recession into a highly successful operation now employing one thousand. One of Driscoll's primary goals, still not accomplished, is to move an appreciable number of Navajos into managerial jobs and one day to see a Navajo take over as plant manager.

AMERICAN METAL CLIMAX. In an effort to reduce the environmental impact of its big molybdenum mine at Henderson, Colorado, AMC launched a unique ecological experiment. The project involved tunneling through a mountain and building a thirteen-mile railroad so that the mill and tailing pond could be built away from public view. As one publication reports, "the mine has become a motherlode of expertise that a dozen companies have tapped." Though far from perfect, the project represents an ambitious, imaginative, and costly contribution of effort, time, and money.

ROUSE COMPANY is cited for its Columbia, Maryland, "new town" established in the countryside between Washington and Baltimore. Especially noteworthy is "the sensitivity and sophistication with which its environmental planning was done." Despite publicity about drug problems, environmental hassles, and a degree of racial conflict, the project is widely described as a "roaring success." The major portion of the plan seems to be working. Columbia now has a fully integrated population of about 35,000 in ten thousand pleasant housing units. It offers more than ten thousand jobs, including twenty-three hundred at General Electric Company's appliance plant and eight thousand at a Bendix research facility. As of June 1973, the town was about one-third of the way toward its goal of 110,000 population in an eminently livable community.

DOZENS MORE

Carborundum Company wins deserved recognition for its efforts toward rehabilitating the rundown city of Niagara Falls, N.Y. With prodigious energy and enthusiasm President William Wendel organized agencies to hammer through an ambitious urban renewal program, stimulate housing, and lay the groundwork for metropolitan government on the Niagara frontier. The work is both rewarding and frustrating, Wendel concedes. Some programs faltered, others succeeded. Wendel devotes about ten hours each month to civic improvement, a significant contribution in view of the host of presidential responsibilities pressing down on him.

The efforts of Campbell Soup Company's president Harold A. Shaub to help refurbish Camden, N.J., are no less frustrating. Camden has the second-highest crime rate in the nation, and parts of it resemble "Dresden after the fire storm." Years of commitment and millions of dollars in special projects and aid for housing development have brought painfully slow progress. Yet Shaub can point to 464 homes rehabilitated in North Camden, as well as construction of 93 low-income town houses, and 104 high-rise apartments.

One new national publication devoted exclusively to social issues, conducts a quarterly review of notable company achievements and failures in areas of public concern.

Among corporate actions cited: Atlantic Richfield Company, in an effort to reduce Los Angeles freeway traffic, is helping to subsidize a commuter bus service for its employees. Six bus lines were set up, running from outlying areas to the Atlantic Richfield Plaza in downtown Los Angeles. ARCO employees pay $25 a month for the round-trip service, with the company footing the $15 balance.

AT&T's Bell Laboratories research arm sponsors a scholarship program to encourage more minorities to enter engineering. It provides outstanding students with full tuition and living expenses during the year and summertime employment at Bell Labs. Eight students are accepted into the program each year. This is the fourth work–study program for minorities initiated by Bell Labs.

Bristol-Meyers Company made one of the largest single grants ever received by public television—$675,000 to underwrite a five-part documentary series on the medical conditions that cause three out of every four deaths in the United States today.

International Business Machines Company has launched a unique program to support community services. Any IBM employee who works in a community organization requiring financial support can apply to the company for it. The request needs only two approvals—the employee's supervisor and one other IBM executive. Since inaugurating its Fund for Community Service in the fall of 1972, IBM has made grants to more than 650 projects in forty-four states (as of the summer of 1973). Nine out of every ten requests from employees have been approved.

In 1973, Hoffman-La Roche, Inc., ran an advertisement in *The New York Times* to present "a progress report to our neighbors." The ad emphasized corporate programs in environmental protection and civic affairs. The move was unusual on two counts. Roche is primarily an ethical drug company, and ethical drug producers have not been notably communicative to the general public. Second, the company is a wholly owned subsidiary of a Swiss firm; its shares are not traded on the U.S. stock exchanges and no disclosure of this kind is required. However, Hoffman-La Roche has long evidenced a high degree of social sensitivity. It has a substantial minority employee force in contrast to most other members of its industry. It started an Indigent Patient program in 1962 under which poor patients can receive Roche drugs free of charge. In 1969 it became the first pharmaceutical company to establish expiration dates for all of its products. In 1972 Roche formed a new department of social issues to spur the company's efforts in minority employment, drug abuse prevention, and other areas of social significance.

Marriott Corporation maintains a strong Career Progression program to advance minorities into responsible positions. About 40 percent of its 11,200 employees are minority members, roughly 70 percent of these in low-rated service jobs. But nearly 10 percent of Marriott's officials and managers are minorities, and nearly 20 percent of its sales employees are black women. "The Real Issue," a sensitivity training seminar on minority affairs, is mandatory for all management trainees. To support minority enterprise, Marriott has made deposits in four minority-owned banks.

Nor have the nation's more progressive banks lagged in their social involvement. Bank of America as far back as 1970 opened a branch in the Watts ghetto in Los Angeles, the first bank to open there since 1918. In New York, Chase Manhattan Bank runs mini–model cities programs in three deteriorating neighborhoods. Bankers Trust Company has 1,600 Vietnam veterans, 160 of them severely disabled, among its 9,500 employees. United Virginia Bankshares, Inc., works with Norfolk's Old Dominion University to create a research and educational center on fifty thousand acres in the Great Dismal Swamp.

In 1970, International Paper Company announced a $101 million program designed to protect the environment at all of its mills and plants, an estimate that has since risen to $145 million, with $120 million approved to date. And Weyerhaeuser Corporation took a full page ad in *Time* to announce that in 1973 it will plant two trees for every family in America. The plan calls for an average planting of about 275,000 seedlings per day on Weyerhaeuser lands.

### Senate Stirrings

In January 1972 Senator Frank Moss of Utah, chairman of the Senate Commerce Consumer Subcommittee, sent an unusual invitation to the first 300 companies on Fortune's 500 list. His letter stated in part:

> One of the persistent criticisms leveled at consumer advocates—both in and out of Government—is that, while roundly scoring the flaws of business, we fail to give credit for the good consumer protections which business performs. In a poll of consumer attitudes reported by *Advertising Age*, Lou Harris found, for example, that while the overwhelming proportion of those polled favored stronger governmental controls over business practices, the majority equally decried the failure of consumer leaders to give credit where credit is due. There is justice in this allegation. As Chairman of the Senate Consumer Subcommittee, I have become increasingly convinced that it is our responsibility to take steps to remedy this gap in the fabric of consumerism.
>
> I would, therefore, like to offer you and your company the opportunity to tell us (in form suitable for printing in a Commerce Committee document) those steps which your company has taken voluntarily to meet the increasing demands of consumers. We are interested in learning how the market system can respond without legislation to meet the increasingly strenuous demands for socially responsible market and production practices. . . .

Out of the 300 invitations, only 181 replied, and not all of them cooperatively. This comes as something of a jolt. I discussed earlier the alternatives facing corporate leaders today regarding social involvement: Take constructive action voluntarily, or wait for action to be legislated. I know of no chief executive who would opt for government mandates over reasonable responsiveness that would make restrictions unnecessary. Laissez faire lamentations long have been echoing from corporate chambers across this land. It is thus a puzzlement that 100 percent of the companies didn't reply vociferously and enthusiastically in an effort to convince legislators that, yes indeed, "the market system *can* respond without legislation to meet the increasingly strenuous demands for socially responsible market and production practices."

On the positive side, several respondents did spell out impressive achievement in hard and concrete terms. In the subcommittee's "Staff Analysis of the Responses," some of the more unique contributions are highlighted.

Among those cited is DelMonte Company's safety warning on cans about the potential hazards of sharp, raw-edge lids, and H. J. Heinz Company's pioneering efforts to ensure safe sealing of baby food containers. Recycling and reclamation campaigns of Reynolds Metal Company, Alcoa, National Can Corporation, and others were commended. The analysis also notes that, "except for an outstanding report submitted by Phillip Morris, Inc., companies engaged in the manufacture of cigarettes declined to participate."

National Distillers and Chemical Corporation got high marks for shifting to low sulphur fuels in its power plants to combat air pollution. Several companies were credited for improved labeling practices. Illinois Central Railroad Company's safety and fire prevention programs received special recognition. So did Avis Rent-A-Car's Driver Education Program conducted in cooperation with the Highway Safety Foundation. General Electric Company's Consumer's Institute was cited for its nationwide workshops on better approaches to cooking and other household tasks.

Motorola, Inc., GE, Merck & Company, and Sunbeam Corporation were among those praised for improved communications systems in response to complaints and queries regarding product and service performance. Flintkote Corporation, American Motors Corporation, O. M. Scott & Sons Company, and Corning Glass Company were commended for informative, consumer-oriented advertising practices. Abbot Laboratories offers through its Ross Laboratories Division free counsel to hospitals to assist in the planning of pediatric wards. It also produces free medical films on surgery, cell life, hospital procedures, and related topics. Schering-Plough Corporation maintains a permanent staff assigned the responsibility of answering questions from medical personnel about the proper use of prescription products. Its Plough division has opened a telephone line for both doctors and laymen to obtain prompt information about medical problems.

Many farsighted chief executives seized upon Senator Moss's invitation as a fine opportunity to air their company's views—and programs—relating to the vital issue of consumer responsibility. E. I. duPont de Nemours & Company, long a pioneer of ambitious social programs too numerous to detail here, discussed its safety, quality, and pollution control programs. It also pioneered consumer protection legislation, most notably the Textile Fiber Products Identification Act requiring most textile products to bear labels showing their fiber content by percentages.

Westinghouse Corporation described its Human Factors Engineering Program, designed "to make use in a more effective and organized way the benefits of consumer surveys, home tests, recommendations of home economists and other sources of suggestions in the formulation of guidelines in the design of products." Key personnel at Westinghouse receive human engineering training at the University of Michigan to help ensure consideration of the consumer at every level of product planning and design.

## Packaged Servility?

Notes establishment critic Charles Reich, "For most Americans work is mindless, exhausting, boring, servile and hateful, something to be endured while 'life' is confined to 'time off.' "

The indictment is more than vituperative venom. Evidence abounds—most dramatically in the auto industry—that if employees could choose between doing their jobs and almost anything else, most would do anything else; not only rank-and-filers—supervisors, sales personnel, and executives as well. In fact, work dissatisfaction was the chief reason General Motors senior executive John Z. De Lorean split from a $500,000-a-year job that he found to be stultifying.

Further evidence of the substance behind Reich's indictment lies in the "thirty and out" labor battle that raged for years between auto unions and management. The demand is that after thirty years on the job an employee be permitted to opt out under full retirement benefits. The operational word is "out."

The nation's most forward-thinking managements, GM among them, have become increasingly sensitive that what's good for people is good for business as well. Job dissatisfaction works the devil with productivity. It triggers crippling absenteeism, high job turnover, poor quality, labor grievances, and strikes. In one recent year alone Chrysler Corporation experienced personnel turnover of 44,000 out of a 100,000 person work force. Early in 1973 GM chairman Richard C. Gerstenberg pinpointed personnel development as "the most important part of our business." Every problem we have, he added, gets back to what I call a people problem.

Worker frustration and dissatisfaction may well be the nation's number one social problem since it involves so many millions of people. Is the problem realistically solvable? A growing number of social-minded—and profit-minded—business leaders think the answer is yes.

To help tackle the "people problem" GM hired former Harvard Business School professor Stephen H. Fuller as vice president of personnel organization and development. The main thrust of his job is "Organization Development" (OD)—a behavioral science method geared to improving the way people work together.

Nor is GM alone in its steps to upgrade job interest and stem worker frustration. In socially sensitive Xerox Corporation's Information Technology Group, for example, an executive function outside the corporate chain of command is in effect to deal objectively with employee problems and complaints. The new employee relations manager fulfills an ombudsman role. Says ITG President James P. O'Neill: "If the firstline manager handles a situation poorly but fills out the forms neatly, by the time this gets four levels up the organization, nobody can tell what's wrong."

Awareness of the need for such response is not symbolic of a new awakening. A widespread movement long has been under way in western Europe to combat worker alienation and job dissatisfaction.

Notes *New York Times* staff writer David Jenkins: "The European movement goes well beyond the current American efforts to attack the authoritarian and bureaucratic excesses of work through job enrichment, job redesign and worker participation."

Several large and small companies, he adds, such as Shell, Philips, Norsk Hydro, Volvo, and Saab have initiated industrial democratization projects. Superficially similar to some of the more advanced participative techniques used in America, some have shown remarkable results in raising productivity as well as job satisfaction.

He cites Nobo Fabrikker as an example. The Norwegian furniture and equipment producer started with a small experiment in the 1960s. It removed foremen, abolished the conventional assembly line, trained workers to perform a variety of tasks, and allowed them to organize in groups to plan, assign, and schedule work among themselves. The results, in terms of both job satisfaction and productivity, were so positive, says Jenkins, that the methods have since spread through most of the company.

Concerning U.S. efforts, he adds: "Despite the current flurry of interest in participative management, only a tiny minority of companies are applying nonauthoritarian techniques to any appreciable extent. And in some United States companies that have initiated advanced participative methods, executives have attempted—often successfully—to kill off innovations that threaten to upset the orthodox authoritarian structure."

But the flurry, however deceptive, is in some quarters encouraging. Using a technique developed by the University of Michigan's Institute for Social Research, five thousand employees were asked about their job, superiors, and plant life generally. The findings urged executives to listen to employees' ideas and "give them more opportunity to participate in establishing goals and solutions in their work areas, and to stimulate more team efforts."

Such urgings are being heeded by a growing number of progressive managements.

### *The Antidote: Participation*

In General Foods Corporation's Gaines pet food plant a team participation system comparable to the Nobo Fabrikker system described above is in force. Supervisors have been replaced by "team leaders" who function as coaches instead of policemen. Time clocks have been eliminated along with such management privileges as special washrooms and dining rooms. Employees set their own lunch and break periods, do much of their own planning and decision-making. The results are dramatic: productivity increases of as much as 40 percent in some departments, absenteeism at an all-time low, employee turnover negligible.

At Motorola, Inc., a motivational program called TEAM stresses employee involvement, individual recognition, and open communication lines to management. It is credited with boosting productivity 30 percent, attendance 95 percent, and chopping labor turnover 25 percent.

Ralston Purina Company's Operations Improvement program has worked so well for four years, according to the company, it is now being marketed to other firms on a fee basis. The system stresses individual involvement and profitability. It makes managers receptive to employee ideas on the one hand, on the other teaches and encourages each worker to be his own problem-solver. OI's key thrust is "to develop a creative environment for our people" with job enrichment in mind.

At Texas Instruments, Inc., a program dubbed "People

and Asset Effectiveness" forces "TI planners to think hard about employees right down to the woman on the assembly line—and about their ability and willingness to produce." According to Mark Shepard, Jr., the company's president and chief executive, "Nobody gets an ulcer from working strenuously at things they like. If you get people involved, they'll set tougher goals." The concept seems to be working. Management attributes a per employee net sales boost of $14,600 in 1970 to $18,500 in 1972 to "a whole bunch of things" which include attitude building techniques, team improvement programs, campus environment, open-door management policy, and nonstructured pecking order.

"It's the unified goal approach," notes Personnel Vice President Frederick C. Ochsner, "with everybody looking at his own piece of that goal." Not all of the programs work equally well. But over-all the effort pays off. The reason, says Ochsner, is simple. There are two things in life that people want, to achieve and to be loved. "If you provide an atmosphere where these things can occur with a minimum amount of structure in the work flow, you are going to get what you want."

## The Case for Confusion

It's hard to debate with confusion. Confusion may well be the strongest argument yet against business voluntarism regarding corporate social involvement.

An imaginative and articulate campaigner for corporate social reform, Charles L. Scarlott, of Exxon Corporation, recently wrote me that the massive problems of society "require coordinated attack based upon decisions—including priority-setting—re which corporate board rooms have neither the mandate nor the capacity. Until they are reasonably well crystallized by society (in law and regulation) there are early practical limits, I think, to business' ability to interpret or act upon them—and there is a danger of good-heartedly riding off in all directions, inefficiently deploying scarce resources." He frankly added, "I am at a loss to conceive how effectively to define, in this pluralistic and divided society, what a 'reasonably prudent, modern, socially conscious management would be expected to undertake.' "

A chief executive friend of mine in the farm machinery business was even more blunt: "What the hell is reasonable?" he asked. "You tell me."

As I pointed out earlier, under SEOS the external audit body of experts would help internal managers to make this determination. But it's not always simple. And, depending on the situation, perplexing problems could arise.

As an executive participant at a 1972 UCLA Business Social Audit Conference stated: "In many instances, corporations won't be able to fulfill the responsibility by themselves. When the corporation participates in the fulfillment of social goals not subject to control within the corporation, the corporation would be well advised to consult with the most relevant agency of the community in deciding what will be helpful in achieving the community's goal. Corporations will be well advised to avoid making solo decisions as to what is good for the community."[1]

Corporate confusion regarding the reasonableness of social responsibility mandates is undoubtedly a prime cause of the spate of federal and state legislative enactments in recent years.

"Since coming to Congress in 1961," notes Senator Richard S. Schweiker, "I have seen many examples of situations where legislation has been required to meet problems which could and should have been met by the business community on its own."

He refers to such bills as Truth in Lending, the Clean Air Act, amendments to the Water Pollution Act, the new safety legislation, the host of new regulations being planned by the fledgling Consumer Product Safety Commission concerning hazardous products.

In June 1971, the senator goes on to say, "the Committee for Economic Development, a top-flight group of senior executives and scholars, adopted a policy statement which set forth some principles and guidelines for corporate and social action. I was particularly interested to note the recommendation that government should promote business efforts in this area by a program of contracts, loans and subsidies for social programs, and by imposing penalties for socially or environmentally harmful activity."

Innumerable questions exist regarding the how-tos and wherefores of corporate social responsibility. Untold problems crop up at every juncture. Perplexities build on perplexities so that confusion reigns supreme.

Clearly a centralized coordinating and integrating body supplemented by subbodies at local levels is needed to spell out relevant social goals and set into motion the machinery of achievement. With this critical national priority in mind, I respectfully suggest the establishment of a peace production board.

### PEACE PRODUCTION BOARD

On December 7, 1941, Pearl Harbor was attacked by Japan. America was at war.

Weeks later President Roosevelt formed the War Production Board. Its purpose was to mobilize the nation's resources for the total war effort. From thousands of plants poured the materials of war in a massive production planning and coordination effort unprecedented in the history of mankind. All sectors of society took part: industry and labor, agencies of government, the academic and scientific communities. All mental and physical resources were directed toward a single objective: the war and its needs. Hundreds of boards and committees were set up to cope with specialized problems and product requirements from munitions and oil to bathtubs and newsprint.

The work week was stretched to forty-eight hours. Factories operated around the clock. Contracts were shifted. Restrictions were set, then shuffled and rearranged in pace with changing product needs.

The Axis war production effort had started rolling a decade ahead of Pearl Harbor. Yet within one year's time, the United States had caught up. By 1943 we were far in advance. The rest of the story is spelled out in your history book.

America's potential for unsurpassed achievement in the face of mind-boggling challenge has been demonstrated repeatedly—in times of war, during the Great Depression of 1929, in the lunar landing program, and on many other occasions.

Now in the seventies we are confronted with a challenge second to none in our history: the challenge of rooting the ravages of social disease from our cities and ghettos.

Are we capable of once again mobilizing our vast resources of manpower, brainpower, production, and technology toward a goal of such staggering significance its outcome could well determine our survival or downfall? I believe that we can. I believe too that with this effort in mind this administration would be well advised to organize a Peace Production Board.

In concept and design such a board would be similar to the War Production Board that preceded it. The model's on hand. Mobilizing our nation's resources to do battle—this time against the social ills plaguing us—should be easier the second time around.

We are in no less of a war. The problem of this war of the seventies is in many respects similar to the problems of other wars we have fought. We will need a host of production materials ranging from housing and health care facilities to mass transportation and antipollution equipment. We will need massive shiftings and shufflings of manpower in our battle to overcome disease, train the illiterate, bring jobs and renewal to our festering ghettos. We will need imaginative strategies and techniques, tax motivations, financial incentives and disincentives, all designed to make social improvement profitable for corporations and eliminate social abuse damaging to earnings performance.

Following the example of the War Production Board, the Peace Production Board and its functional subagencies would tap the talent and expertise of experts drawn from industry and government, labor and the sciences, academia and the professions.

Mobilizing America's resources for war helped to overcome the evils of totalitarianism and tyranny. A remobilization for peace will conquer with equal effectiveness the evils of social injustice and poverty.

# 10
# "INC. SPOTS"
# OF THE EIGHTIES

The poet William Cowper once wrote, "Spring hangs her infant blossoms on the trees."

We are, when one thinks of it, in the springtime of corporate social responsibility. The infant blossoms are in the process of being hung. I believe it is safe to say that by the end of this decade we will see a profusion of growth that will seem lush by comparison. The signs are unmistakable.

Notes a business weekly:

> The idea of a corporate social audit has captured the imaginations of social critics, businessmen, consultants, and professional accountants alike. Such groups as the Council on Economic Priorities, the National Council of Churches' Corporate Information Center, and the student-led Committee for Corporate Responsibility all have tried their hands at auditing individual companies' social performance in the areas of minority hiring, defense contracting, or pollution. A number of mutual funds, including the Dreyfus Third Century Funds, have been launched with the policy of investing only in what are deemed to be "socially responsible companies," based on the fund managers' assessment of social performance.
>
> On the business front, management consultants such as Arthur D. Little, Inc., have been helping clients

work on social audits, and the American Institute of Certified Public Accountants appointed a committee to help develop "standards and techniques for measuring, recording, reporting, and auditing social performance."

## The Corporate Hotfoot

The racist white manager of a midwest supermarket was recently fired after fifteen years with the company. The reason, his obstinate refusal to hire black or nonwhite workers for other than the most low-rated menial jobs despite repeated requests from headquarters that he "do something about balancing the ratio."

A district supervisor of this major chain expressed off-the-record relief at the dismissal. "The guy hardly made a pretense," he said. "I shudder to think of the consequences we so narrowly escaped. We could have been impaled in the marketplace as a result of his blatant prejudice."

What he no doubt referred to was the action that might have been—and probably would have been—instituted by a local citizens' group against unfair labor practices. Less than a decade ago only a handful of organizations formed to monitor corporate social performance existed. Today they are numbered in the hundreds, their membership of concerned citizens in the hundreds of thousands. Specific interests range from the environment, military–industrial complex, and foreign investments to consumer rights, public health and safety, labor and minority practices.

The Corporate Information Center of the National Council of Churches in an October 1971 report includes a highlight sampling of well over a hundred major groups. "The organizations noted here," states CIC, "do not represent a total account of groups addressing themselves to the problems generated by business organizations. There are also numerous local groups which receive little publicity and national attention, but are involved in day-to-day struggle to influence corporate policies."

Typical of groups listed in the rundown is New York's Citizens for Clean Air, a research and action group "working against pollution through attacking the automobile, the incinerator and oil burner, and the power plant." Washington, D.C.'s Conservation Foundation has "helped set up local Coalitions for Clean Air in many metropolitan areas to increase citizen participation in the implementation of the Air Quality Control Act of 1967. These coalitions now form a solid base for further work on the 1970 amendments."

Chicago's Anti-Imperialism Conference is "involved in antiwar activity, support of liberation movements, and research on U.S. corporations in the Third World." Operation Breadbasket consists of hundreds of Protestant and Roman Catholic clergymen who negotiate agreements with food chains, soft drink firms, dairies, and other companies to make jobs available for blacks. National Organization for Women (NOW) engages in various types of actions protesting discrimination against women. The purpose of Brain Mistrust, Ann Arbor, Michigan, is "to make the corporations serve all the people, not just the upper class." It suggests grassroots actions appropriate to specific problems in local communities. Ralph Nader's Center for the Study of Responsive Law promotes citizen–consumer interest before the regulatory agencies, courts, legislatures, and individual corporations. A satellite Corporate Accountability Research Group "examines antitrust problems as well as the adequacy of government prosecution of corporate crime."

Other names imply the degree of concern and determination involved: Businessmen for the Public Interest, Citizen's Action Program, Friends of the Earth, Environmental Action, Inc., Project Equality, Health Policy Advisory Center, Center for New Corporate Priorities, National Affiliation of Concerned Business Students.

The proliferation of such groups isn't likely to flag in the foreseeable future. For one thing the media—oral, visual, and printed—have enlisted in the war against social irresponsibility on all fronts. Media exposure inevitably fuels public interest and indignation. Thus politicians, sensitive to constituent sensitivities, altruistically or not, also have joined in the watchdogging.

One official states it, "Around election time the way a candidate responds to the social concerns of his constituency can put him well ahead in the race or hang a noose around his neck. I could cite half a dozen shrewd campaigners who unseated well entrenched incumbents primarily because of their aggressive stance on a crucial social issue."

The indicators are clear and unmistakable. In the early sixties a comparative handful of citizens participated aggressively in social research and action. The early seventies witnessed an exponential expansion. By 1980 we may have monitors to monitor the monitors and watchdogs to watchdog the watchdogs.

### Student Power

On May 16, 1973, five business school graduate students were clustered on the campus of a prestigious eastern college discussing prospects and plans for the future.

One bright young man who ranked near the top of his class was asked, "How'd you make out with that interview?"

His interview the day before had been with one of the nation's largest insurance companies headquartered in the East.

"I was offered the job."

"How much?"

He named an impressive figure. He quickly added, "I turned it down."

Eyebrows were raised. "How come?"

"Well, here's one of the reasons." He produced a copy of a report by a reputable national publication on corporate social performance by leading U.S. companies. The insurance company that interviewed him had been cited in the report for a variety of social abuses. The student read aloud to the others a report that Florida's insurance commissioner, Thomas O'Malley, had informed the company its advertising was misleading and demanded that it be kept out of the state. It further noted that the company, which had pledged "it would not turn its back on its headquarters city," continued to transfer personnel out of the beleagured metropolis now headed by a black mayor.

The MBA candidate slapped shut the report. An active member of the National Affiliation of Concerned Business Students, he met the eyes of his friends. "I don't think I'd be happy working for that kind of an outfit. Would you?"

Admittedly, this was an exceptional young man, but his kind appears to be increasing. Recent evidence as well as personal experience as visiting professor at the University of Illinois indicates that among current student crops, salary is only one of the major factors that determine employment decisions.

In 1972 a survey questionnaire was mailed to the placement directors of the 243 graduate business schools listed in the Graduate Business Administration Council's 1971–1972 directory. A 50 percent return was received. Placement directors were asked: "Assuming that the [MBA] student had at least one other reasonable job offer, what percentage of your students do you think would refuse to work for a company against which pollution suits have been filed by the U.S. government?" The mean response was 15 percent. Another 15 percent wouldn't work for a company engaged in the manufacture of antipersonnel weapons.

Twenty-four percent would refuse employment with a company that was regularly cited by the FTC for false and misleading advertising. Fifteen percent would turn down job offers from a company consistently cited by the EEOC for discriminatory hiring practices against racial minorities, 12 percent if the charge was discriminatory practices against women.

Realistically, student concern over corporate social performance fluctuates as the job market ranges from strong to weak. But generally, more than 80 percent of the director respondents believe that MBAs today are more concerned with the social effects of business than they were ten years ago. "Changes in student attitudes have not gone unnoticed by corporate recruiters," the survey report notes. "Eighty-eight percent of our respondents agreed that, as compared with ten years ago, recruiters today demonstrate greater concern with the social effect of their companies. Sixty-one percent felt this concern has continued to increase during the last two [weak job market] years."

The report adds, "All of our data pertain to students who are currently in business schools. One important factor not revealed by such data is the number of students who do not even enter business school because of their negative perceptions of the social responsibility record of business. A substantial number of our respondents alluded to this phenomenon."[1]

In the spring of 1973 the National Affiliation of Concerned Business Students mailed questionnaires to 272 graduate business schools. The aim was to determine the extent to which students are being taught how to formulate and implement corporate social policy. One hundred and sixteen schools, or 43 percent of those polled, responded. Of these 18 percent said they had no courses on corporate social policy, 45 percent offered one course, 37 percent two or more courses. The larger the school, the more likely it was to have multiple course offerings and plans to expand social coverage.

A leading publisher of educational materials told me recently, "Any management that fails to take the pulse of today's enlightened business student is operating in a vacuum, for it is here that tomorrow's leaders will be tapped."

As this century draws to a close student power will work increasingly to influence corporate decisions and bring social activist pressures to bear on business. It also might be well to remember that today's student is not only tomorrow's business leader, he's tomorrow's customer, supplier, and the consumer as well.

What is he learning in school? Current course titles are revealing. Typical of one graduate school's offerings: "Contemporary Issues and Management Responsibility," "Socio-Economic Accountability," "Problems of Administration in Changing Environments," "Business Leadership and Urban Problems." A random sampling of others: "The Interaction of Business and Government," "Public Services and Private Functions," "Business and Society," "Law and the Changing Environment," "Business and Its Urban Environment," "Corporate Behavior and the Public Interest," "Ethics and Business," "Black Power and the Business Community," "Socio-Economic Accounting," "The Social Setting of Business," "Responsibilities of Business Leadership," "Doctoral Seminar in Business, Government, and Society."

A decade ago such courses were rare. Today Boston College offers five of them, Carnegie Mellon University eight, UCLA six, New York University nine, University of Washington twelve. A decade ago the professor who specialized in social issues was something of a maverick. Today it's not uncommon to find seven or eight professors at a major college listed under such headings as Urban Affairs or Corporate Social Policy.

A harbinger of things to come?

The trend would be hard to ignore. It would not surprise me if by 1980 the BSI (Bachelor of Social Improvement) degree were almost as common as the BBA, BA, and BS degree are today.

## Investor Power

A friend of mine is a group vice president of a large company that produces industrial machinery. A few months ago we lunched at New York's Pinnacle Club. He appeared tired and harassed.

"Problems?" I asked.

He winced. "Is it that obvious?"

He went on to explain. His company's annual stockholder meeting was scheduled for the following week.

"Isn't that pretty much routine?"

"Not this year."

The problem he described was a recent management decision to discontinue a minority training program the company had launched the previous year. "It's costly as the devil and not working out as we hoped. But I can feel in my bones that chopping it was a bad decision. It may cost us more in the end than seeing it through, despite the difficulties."

"How's that?"

"We'll be clobbered at that meeting. We've been holding sessions all week in an effort to find a reasonable way to cope with the attack we'll inevitably get. No way exists. We made promises and commitments we haven't kept and I'm afraid we won't get away with it. The damage to our reputation may take years to live down. We tried to get this across to the board, but they voted us down."

Investor power!

The so-called corporate gadfly is by no means new on the business scene. But never before has his clout been so formidable. Nor does an investor need a substantial investment to make his presence felt. All it takes is a few shares of stock, a cause, and a voice.

"In addition to the carefully organized and widely publicized Campaign GM," notes lawyer Joel F. Henning, a consultant to the Corporate Accountability Research Group, "some form of attention has been called to social problems at the recent annual meetings of many companies including AT&T (military contracts), Atlantic-Richfield (pollution), Bank of America (Vietnam), Boeing (military contracts), Columbia Broadcasting System (women's liberation), Commonwealth Edison (pollution), Dow Chemical (military contracts), General Electric (military contracts, pollution, women's liberation), Gulf (colonial investments), Honeywell (military contracts), IBM (military contracts), Kennecott Copper (pollution), National Tea (consumer protection), Standard Oil of New Jersey (Vietnam), Union Carbide (pollution), and United Aircraft (military contracts)."[2]

Proxy contests over social issues ranging from hiring and safety to weapons production and pollution have been raging like a prairie blaze since the dawn of this decade. The signs all indicate they will continue to proliferate.

Conventional response on the heels of a proxy proposal is corporate protest to the Securities and Exchange Commission that the issue is not a proper one for submission to stockholder vote. But increasingly such proposals are winning SEC approval as presented or in modified form, and more and more votes are taking place. In almost every case the proposal is defeated. But in defeat lies a hard core of victory for the investor dissenter.

As one crusader exultantly exclaimed after a battle to curtail certain corporate transactions in apartheid South Africa: "Realistically, we knew we didn't have a prayer of winning. But the publicity was priceless. It created an awareness we couldn't have produced otherwise. The company has no choice now but to moderate its position accordingly."

One of the most successful shareholder protests to date, and a forerunner of others to follow, was the battle waged against Eastman Kodak in the late 1960s. Dubbed FIGHT (Freedom, Integration, God, Honor, Today), the proxy war was only one of a host of Saul Alinsky–inspired ploys to reform hiring practices. Kodak, socially sensitive to the extreme, responded positively and aggressively.

In 1970 in Chicago a campaign was launched by a group calling itself Campaign Against Pollution (CAP). CAP's primary goal was to pressure the city's major polluter, Commonwealth Edison Company, into substantially reducing its sulfur dioxide emission. Its chief tactic was to collect a number of proxies and to appear at the company's annual meeting. With massive representation, no specific proposals were necessary. Shortly after the meeting, Commonwealth Edison made a commitment to cut the sulfur dioxide content of its fuel to an acceptable level.

## Pressure Groups Under Fire

It would be difficult to refute the argument that a manufacturing company's prime purpose is to earn a profit for its shareholders. For scores of institutions with billions of dollars to invest—most notably churches, universities, foundations, and many pension funds—different objectives exist. The socially oriented organization is increasingly under fire both from within and the community it serves to take positive steps wherever possible to help upgrade the corporate conscience and simultaneously the quality of life.

One major hurdle of the institutional and public service auditor is access to corporate information. But this hurdle appears destined to shrink in size as we pass through this decade and into the next. For one thing, the trend is clearly toward increased government mandating of corporate disclosure requirements. What's more, public's right-to-know pressures are steadily building. Early in 1973, First National City Bank of New York sent a questionnaire on corporate responsibility to sixteen hundred personal trust customers. About 25 percent responded. The overwhelming majority of this group believed corporations *must* present evidence of their social responsibility.

In days to come "must" could well become the operational word. Last summer institutional probers questioned a large metals fabricator about its plans to cut down on pollution. Repeated attempts failed to elicit the desired information. The investor group responded by dumping the company's stock and replacing it with shares of a "more socially responsive corporation."

On the heels of the sale the institution's investment manager received a call from the company's chief executive. "Sorry," the executive was told, "but the matter is closed."

Essentially, what the concerned private and institutional investor wants to know is whether corporations are meeting their social obligations or not. To make this assessment they are getting plenty of help, and will get more as investor-geared auditing services inevitably expand. The Council on Economic Priorities, for example, was established in 1970 to "disseminate unbiased and detailed information on the practices of U.S. corporations. CEP delves into four major areas: minority employment, the environment, military production, and foreign investment. Its in-depth reports compare the performance of various companies within a single industry.

The Investor Responsibility Research Center, Inc. (IRRC), is a nonprofit, Washington-based group created in December 1972 in response to institutional investors' need to know. Sponsored primarily by foundations and universities, it gives clients objective insights into complicated issues and uncovers facts that institutional staffers have neither the time nor expertise to unearth.

IRRC's main function, by its own definition, "is to provide impartial, timely, in-depth analysis concerning corporate social responsibility issues. It does not take positions on issues; it does not make recommendations or become an advocate. Investors, acting individually, continue to have the responsibility for the final evaluation of any issue."

What all this adds up to is a strong case for the Socio-Economic Operating Statement. Clearly institutional, public interest, and social-activist probers do not share the cost and profit concerns of internal managers. Clearly voluntary social reporting would serve corporate interests more advantageously than legislated disclosure of information squeezed from the tube under pressure.

## Good Business

The far-sighted investment analyst more and more equates corporate social responsibility with sound, pragmatic management. Costly as it may be for a corporation to meet its obligations to society fully and honestly, it is often even more costly to sidestep responsibility.

A case in point is a southern chemical company. In 1969 it ploughed $1 million dollars into a new plant complex. In an effort to save money it cut corners on pollution control equipment which would have cost an additional $65,000 at the time the plant was built. In the spring of 1973 the company's general manager was visited by a representative from the Environmental Protection Administration. Several complaints already had been registered regarding pollution of local streams by the company's effluent discharge. The showdown had come. Management was faced with two alternatives: Get rid of the pollution, or shut down.

The company opted to remain in operation. But the price exacted was relatively high. To install control equipment, some of the old equipment was scrapped. On top of this, a rather extensive redesign of systems, procedures, and processing was required. The total cost estimate came to $134,000, more than twice the amount it would have cost had the job been done right in the first place.

It is fashionable these days to talk of corporate social responsibility as an important consideration for the socially minded investor. But it's far more than a fashion or fad, as more than one sophisticated Wall Streeter I know would confirm. Laying plans for the inevitable makes economic good sense for the investor, the community, the national economy in general. The company that cuts social corners today in an effort to hike current earnings performance is no different from the company that unduly delays replacement of outmoded plant or machinery with the same purpose in mind. It should be bypassed by the investor on purely financial grounds. Unwarranted corner cutting applies not only to such obvious areas as safety and pollution control, but to product quality, minority employment, training, plant location, work environment, and other areas as well. Overcoming the sociomyopic syndrome, in short, extends well beyond corporate idealism. It strikes the very lifestream of earnings per share so vital to stockholders and potential investors.

## *Hopes and Realities*

A sprinkling of hopeful signs have become visible in recent years that society as a whole and the investor in particular is coming of age. He is no longer unmindful as he once was of the long-range consequences of corporate social responsibility.

*The Ethical Investor*, by Professor John Simon, published in 1972, serves as a bible on investments for the university community. "Guidelines," prepared by the American Bankers Association, helps bank trust officers to assess the corporate conscience in making investment decisions. The Corporate Information Center publishes its own set of guidelines for churchmen charged with investment responsibility.

The investment community itself has not failed to take notice of the mounting social awareness of private and institutional investors. A scattering of "clean funds" have sprung up in response. Unhappily, they were spawned during a period when common stocks generally and mutual funds especially were singularly unexciting. The largest of the group, Dreyfus Third Century, states in its March 1972 prospectus that it "will invest in companies which not only meet traditional investment standards, but also show evidence in the conduct of their business relative to other companies in the same industry or industries, of contributing to the enhancement of the quality of life in America. . . ."

A handful of smaller socially sensitive funds are also firing miniature darts in an effort to prick the corporate conscience. First Spectrum Fund gauges a company's performance on civil rights, ecology, and consumer protection before buying its shares. After Bohack Corporation, a supermarket chain in New York, signed an agreement with Operation Breadbasket to hire and promote more blacks, First Spectrum bought Bohack shares and urged the fund's shareholders to patronize the grocery chain. Pax World Fund provides an investment vehicle that steers clear of war profiteers. About half of its $450,000 in assets comes from individuals, the rest from foundations and religious organizations. The fund tries to concentrate its holdings in benevolent industries such as housing, food, leisure, pollution control, and health care.

The Wellington Fund, also run by socially concerned managers, asked shareholders their opinion on the following statement: "Even if other companies offer better investment prospects, a mutual fund should invest only in socially responsible companies . . . i.e., those that avoid pollution with their manufacturing plants; those concerned with product safety; those that do not discriminate in their hiring practices." Twenty-eight percent of those surveyed responded. Of these 27.3 percent "strongly agree" and 28.8 percent "generally agree" with the contention. "Not sure," are 11.1 percent, and 32.8 percent disagree.

How firm are the signs? Is it merely a matter of time before the national corporate conscience becomes pure of its own accord? Permitting ourselves to ignore the realities and be lulled by false hopes could prove disastrous.

The opposition to pleas for social involvement is as formidable as ever. One major segment, as I pointed out earlier, is made up of those businessmen who contend that the only business of business is profits and growth. Inside and outside this group are the main body of earnings-obsessed investors who singlemindedly clamor for "performance now," and to hell with the future.

Unquestionably, minor inroads have been made by social-activist groups, concerned students and journalists, conscience-driven investors, and responsible representatives of business, government, and academia. More significant inroads will inevitably be made as pressures and media coverage continue to build and accelerate. It *is* becoming more difficult and less profitable to disregard the corporate conscience when making business decisions and setting company policy. But taken in total context progress has been slow and results microscopic. For the visionary big-picture businessman, it's almost like a building contractor forced to sit helplessly by while his crew uses toy shovels to empty a truckload of sand.

Unhappily too, there are discouraging signs to offset the strides being made. One biweekly report on business and social responsibility, set up its own "Social Responsibility Portfolio," a fourteen-company index of outstandingly conscionable corporations. For comparative purposes it also worked up a dirty dozen plus two of socially irresponsible companies, a portfolio of some of the nation's worst performers in the opinion of the editors. Market performance was logged for the first six months of 1973, a period during which stock market averages were generally down. During the period the Social Responsibility index fell 25 percent while the Irresponsibility index declined only 12.2 percent.

Noted the editor: "When the market turned down early in 1973, the companies we had selected for inclusion in our portfolio were clobbered, much to the glee of Wall Streeters who see social responsibility as a meaningless externality . . . . The biggest beating taken by any stock on either list was the 55 percent dip in the price of Levi Strauss & Co., the San Francisco jeans maker which has long been singled out a pioneer in social responsibility." He adds, "The best performer on either list was the master pill salesman, American Home Products, which split 3-for-1 and managed a 5 percent gain in the face of plunging prices. The maker of Anacin, Preparation H, and Chef-Boy-Ar-Dee canned spaghetti continues to lead a charmed life, unscathed by continual run-ins with the Federal Trade Commission over the manner in which it promotes its products."

Another somber note is added by Harvey D. Shapiro: "After more than a year of operation, the nation's three social responsibility funds are not doing terribly well, nor have they done much good."

Most professional investment managers, claims Shapiro, who is a fellow at New York's Russell Sage Foundation and a contributing editor of the *Institutional Investor*, denied they had a right, much less a duty to be more than passive investors, while others gradually accepted the notion of

194

responsibility but weren't quite sure what they were supposed to do about it. As Donald Weeden, chairman of Weeden & Company, a brokerage concern, told the *Institutional Investor* three years ago, "There are hundreds of people in our industry looking for a vehicle to do in a responsible way what they think Ralph Nader may be doing in an irresponsible way."

The appeal for responsible responsiveness is one we hear sounded more and more these days by pragmatic and conscionable businessmen, government leaders, academicians, and more enlightened investors.

### Nation of Scorekeepers

One of the questions most frequently asked of the editor of a newly established business oriented publication is, "Which are the best companies?"

We are a society of contestants, a nation of scorekeepers. We have a burning curiosity to know who's in the lead and who's in the cellar.

Recently there was a listing of America's "most socially responsible corporations" based on two publications' studies and on three different public opinion surveys that began in 1971.

A senior vice president of a major U.S. airline told me recently that the company's chief executive had called a meeting of his high-level aides in which he bluntly demanded, "Why the hell isn't our name on that list?"

Top executives in most small companies are usually so time-pressured by day-to-day crises and priorities that they shove social responsibility into dark recesses of their minds. But many heads of large and medium-sized corporations experience personal stirrings of conscience if not sharp pangs. More pragmatically, they harbor vague feelings that their companies will be hurt in the long run if the stirrings are ignored. However, as Harvey Shapiro points out, those who are honestly and consciously concerned aren't "quite sure what they're supposed to do about it," on the one hand, and on the other so pressured by the performance hawks, they wind up doing nothing.

But this situation is destined to change. It is becoming increasingly hard for the large, highly visible, publicly held corporation to remain inured to its social obligations. As the scorekeeping multiplies and the pressures continue to build, concerned chief executives, especially in consumer-oriented companies, inevitably will look more searchingly at the corporate profile. The trend will accelerate as the benefits of favorable public exposure and the potential harm of poor citizenship ratings and accusations grow more and more apparent.

The Dow Chemical Company is a good case in point. It was so concerned over adverse publicity generated by its decision to supply napalm for the Indo-China war, that it has gone overboard in its efforts to live down this image. In recent years Dow has achieved nationwide recognition for its pioneering efforts to combat air and water pollution. So far has it come since the dirty dark days of the napalm decision that it was cited in a recent national publication as one of the nation's thirty-nine "most socially responsible corporations."

## The Anvil Chorus

A pile driver in your backyard would be hard to ignore. Hammer away incessantly at the masses with heavy barrages of publicity and it will force people to think and draw conclusions whether they want to or not. It would be difficult to find an American today so indifferent to the environment as to be unaware of the devastating effects of pollution on our quality of life.

Millions of New Yorkers, Chicagoans, inhabitants of major cities from Pittsburgh to San Francisco and Savannah to Los Angeles suffer from respiratory problems, eye irritations, and heart impairment brought on by dirty, sulfur-and soot-laden air. These people are customers and consumers. They care—if not for society, for their personal well-being.

On March 28, 1973, the Sierra Club took a full-page ad in *The New York Times.* On top was depicted a face, eyes tearing from the city smog and grime. Below the heading, addressed to the then administrator of the Environmental Protection Administration, read: "Dear Mr. Ruckelshaus: How many tears must we shed from the poisonous sting before our eyes will open? It's springtime in the city and oh, for a taste of clean, fresh air."

I watched a man read this ad in the lobby of a New York hotel. He muttered something under his breath and slapped the newspaper hard against a chair in a rage.

This man was concerned.

If in the weeks ahead he happened to see or hear that XYZ Corporation had been charged by the EPA as a polluter, he'd be likely to remember—and to exercise his memory when confronted by XYZ's products or services. More and more today's citizens appear to be reading and hearing and remembering. The far-sighted corporate leader is responding to this hopeful phenomenon. Increasingly he is coming to realize that good corporate citizenship is not only conscionable behavior, it's good business as well.

When students demonstrate against a company for producing antipersonnel weapons, the pragmatic executive understands it will generate hostility among a percentage of consumers, employees, and potential recruits.

When a proxy fight is waged against a retail chain for discriminatory hiring practices, the pragmatic executive understands it will fuel labor unrest and turn off some shoppers.

When a company is publicly tarred for polluting the air, for its dehumanized work environment, for robbing the terrain of its natural scenic values, the pragmatic executive understands that some customers will switch to a competitor's products, some job candidates will think twice before seeking employment there, some investors will reconsider decisions regarding their funds.

## Increasing Involvement

However haltingly and uncertainly, more corporations than ever are using their money in an effort to give society a boost instead of a blemish.

Former U.S. Attorney-General Nicholas Katzenbach, now serving as an executive officer and director of IBM, stresses the need for what he refers to as a "greening of the board room." What he calls for specifically is for corporations to issue a policy statement on social responsibility designed to show clearly and unmistakably what the board's position really is. He further recommends that a committee be created to periodically assess corporate behavior against prestated intention. Several large corporations already have formulated policy statements and set up high-level monitoring committees bearing such titles as "committee on social responsibility," or "public affairs committee."

Many companies, notes The Conference Board, go a giant step further in not only allowing but encouraging employee involvement in social and political activities. One form this encouragement takes is a liberalized leave-of-absence policy, formal or informal. To assess the extent of such practices, the Board polled eight hundred of the *Fortune* one thousand companies.

Thirty-four percent responded. Of these 28 percent have formal policies covering employee participation in political and social activities, while 17 percent have informal (unwritten) policies. Thirty percent handle each request on an individual basis. Ten percent do not now have a formal policy on this subject but are considering adopting one. Six percent report that they are opposed to any such policy; and 9 percent say that the question of a leave for political or social reasons has never been raised in their companies.

In addition to granting leaves of absence, some companies are seeking, through volunteer pools, time off with pay, and other means, to make political and social activities part of the normal job responsibility.[3]

The trend appears destined to grow. IBM had over one hundred employees on leave during 1972. One man was David Evans, an electronics engineer at the company's Huntsville, Alabama, plant. The son of a sharecropper, Evans managed to work his way through Tennessee State College and Princeton University. He emerged with an understanding of what a black deprived youngster must go through to attain this objective. Now on his second two-year leave of absence, his mission is to awaken the aspirations of black students to attend college. Serving as an assistant director of placement at Harvard, he finds the work gratifying. After all, Evans says, "the end product is a human being."

Another IBMer who cares about the human end product is forty-seven-year-old Robert S. Lee, a specialist in sophisticated learning techniques at the company's Armonk, New York, headquarters. During a year's paid leave, Lee put his expertise at the service of New York's Economic Development Council which seeks new approaches to teaching ghetto youngsters. At the Bronx's James Monroe High School, a predominantly black and Puerto Rican school, Lee set up simulation games like Make Your Own World, Word Power, and Starpower.

Lee's successor at Monroe High, a volunteer from First National City Bank, became quickly involved in studying the possibility of training simulation teaching teams to conduct sessions throughout the school system on a "floating" basis.

It's my conviction that the large majority of this nation's business executives are as conscionable as they are pragmatic. They honestly would like to make socially responsible decisions and set corporate policy beneficial to mankind. I believe this augurs well for the state of the corporate conscience in decades to come.

The crucial factor is time. We have waited too long already, and have come up with too many alibis for postponing the resolute action required to turn society around. Fool around too much with the fire hose and the barn will burn down.

All most businessmen really need, I believe, is the guidance, direction, and controls to ensure that the burden and restructuring of social reform will be divided fairly and practically among individual companies within each industry. In short, they want to be sure that neither they nor their companies will be unduly penalized for acting socially responsible, and that competitors will not gain an unfair marketplace edge by failing to shoulder their share of the social burden and cost.

When you boil it down, this basically is what the social measurement and reporting system is all about.

# 11
# SOCIAL REPORTING: A ONE-WAY STREET

Last year a large producer of heavy industrial equipment was experiencing serious labor problems in its main plant. All the classical symptoms were present, from excessive absenteeism and work rejects to high employee turnover and low productivity. An employee behavioral specialist was brought in to review the situation.

The consultant went into the plant, talked with managers, supervisors, rank and file workers. He encouraged them to speak openly, promising complete anonymity.

Afterward, he revealed his findings to the president of the company. "Morale," he explained, was "dangerously low."

"That's not news to me," the president responded. "But why?"

The consultant informed the chief executive that one conversation with a line foreman had been particularly revealing and, in his opinion, representative of sentiments throughout the company. The foreman's exact words: "Nobody gives a damn around here!"

Asked to elaborate, he shrugged and cited examples he clearly felt strongly about. High-level executives were under investigation by the SEC for what he described as "shady operations." The company had been charged by the Environmental Protection Administration with several counts of polluting the atmosphere. A few months back, he added, a middle manager who had been with the company twenty-two years was fired when the operation he had been in charge of was discontinued. His pension entitlement was cut off.

"The man's fifty-seven years old," the foreman said. "The work he did was all he knows. What's he supposed to do now?"

When the foreman complained that "nobody gives a damn," in essence he was talking about morality and ethics, social responsibility.

The consultant's point was this: Where an organization's leadership fails to demonstrate responsibility in its policies, dealings, and decisions, how can it expect lower ranking employees to perform responsibly? Inevitably, irresponsibility at the top must be reflected in poor work habits and reduced productivity throughout the operation.

Few students of business would argue that the key word for corporate success in tomorrow's economy is increased productivity. As in the case cited above, large corporations like General Motors and American Telephone & Telegraph Company have been investing massive resources for years in an effort to understand the root causes of worker dissatisfaction and frustration.

It appears clear that at least some of the problem is attributable to the nature of the "work itself," and to this whole broad matter of ethics and morality.

General Electric Company's Ian H. Wilson must have had this partly in mind when he said, "I think we must recognize that there is a real danger of a potential discontinuity in productivity improvement rates . . . . It seems to me there *is* an aspect of the 'quality of life' issue that ties in with the quality of work."

What impact does corporate social irresponsibility have on productivity and work performance? I have long pondered this question. In a previous chapter I proposed the organization of an American Peace Production Board patterned after the War Production Board that operated so successfully during World War II.

Now I would further recommend, along with Dean C. Jackson Grayson, Jr., of Southern Methodist University's School of Business Administration, a nonprofit organization, funded and operated by the private sector, to focus solely on increasing American productivity and to be called the American Productivity Institute. It does not take a great deal of imagination to visualize API as a working arm of the Peace Production Board. As one of its functions, a responsibility of the API would be to study the impacts of social irresponsibility on U.S. productivity.

As Dean Grayson notes: "Japan has developed such an organization, the privately run Japan Productivity Center, a 300-man educational, data-gathering, research, informational, and counseling organization for both labor and management. It has a $7.5 million annual budget, which was originally—and ironically—set up by foreign aid and U.S. experts. West Germany has a productivity center, the RFK, with a staff of 500. Even tiny Israel has developed a 400-man Israel Institute of Productivity.

"But the U.S., which is still the most powerful and productive nation on earth, has only a 20-man National Commission on Productivity in Washington, whose annual working budget is about $2.5 million, an insignificant amount in a $250 billion national budget."

### Partners for Progress

*The Time:* April 1943. *The Place:* A manufacturing plant in Ohio. The telephone rings on Jim's desk, the president.

FRED: Jim, I was just on the line with Detroit. They're behind schedule on those light-duty field vehicles.

JIM: What seems to be the problem?

FRED: They're not getting the delivery they need on tandem drive units and the number four assemblies.

JIM: Pittsburgh?

FRED: Right. I talked with Pittsburgh, too. The complaint there is that the carbide drills, high speed taps and dies, and some other needed tools aren't coming through. They've been using unsatisfactory substitutes and running into excessive downtime as a result. That's where you come into the picture. What can you do about getting them the stuff they need?

JIM: We're running full speed around the clock now, Fred. It's a matter of reshuffling priorities.

FRED: Then let's reshuffle. Those vehicles are desperately needed. The Pentagon has been hot on my tail. We're going to have to get that stuff moving.

JIM: I couldn't agree more. Can we sit down and resolve it?

FRED: Sure thing, Jim. I'll fly down there tomorrow.

The meeting was held the following afternoon. By the time it was over, the problem was resolved.

An unusual show of aggressive action and swift decision-making? Today, perhaps. But not thirty years ago.

"Fred," as you may have surmised, was an official at a subunit of the War Production Board. Serving as liason man between government and business, his responsibility was to see to it that the job got done right and on time. World War II's production effort has been described by historians as "the most massive and complex organization of resources ever attempted by man." That the United States was able in a prodigiously short time to catch up with and surpass Axis production is dramatic proof of the effort's success.

The phenomenon was duplicated years later in Project Apollo. In this mammoth enterprise thousands of industrial prime and subcontractors worked in close cooperation with government administrators and watchdogs to get a man on the moon ahead of schedule.

If government-business partnership can help win a war and land a space ship on the moon, it can help solve problems of social restructuring.

One thing is certain. Government can't do it alone. Business can't do it alone. The War Production Board was effective because a diversity of disciplines and expertise was

applied to the problems at hand. Project Apollo was successful for precisely the same reason.

We should have learned by now that you can't run a ball
club with nine shortstops on the field. Specific responsibilities require specific training and experience. Diagnosis
and prescription relating to dread diseases of society require
a spirited pooling of human and technical resources if the
job's to get done.

Industry is in a uniquely fine position to aid and advise
government on establishing and achieving acceptable standards relating to life style, work, health care, the ecology,
and other social areas.

Why don't we see more of the kind of government–business partnership for progress that worked so well during
World War II and America's space program? Partly
because we keep deferring action until the "facts are all in."

All the facts will never be in.

But partnership leanings are trending upward. A dedicated and influential core of business and government
leaders perceived the potential that exists if the two sectors
pool their talents and experience. During the past decade
some slow but clear progress has been made in joint efforts
to teach "unemployables" new skills, aid minority enterprise, and refurbish U.S. ghettos.

The partnership trend, sometimes called "privatizing"
the public sector, reflects a growing acceptance of four important propositions, according to the Committee for Economic Development.

1. That the goals of American Society can be realized
only through a massive, cooperative effort of government,
industry, labor, and education. Increasingly it is felt that
the cooperative participation of the private sector is required not only for national defense and space exploration
but also for advances in health care, improvement of education, and elimination of poverty.

2. That government's basic role through the political process is to determine the nation's goals, set the priorities,
develop the strategies, and create the conditions for carry-

ing out the work most effectively to the satisfaction of the public.

3. That business, with its profit-and-loss discipline, has an especially significant role in the actual execution of social programs because it is a proven instrument for getting much of society's work done and because its top executives, with their diverse management capabilities and their involvement in community affairs, are normally well fitted to deal with today's socio-economic problems.

4. That the incentive for profit is the only practicable way of unleashing the power and dynamism of private enterprise on a scale that will be effective in generating social progress. Social consciousness and good citizenship, while important prerequisites, cannot realistically be expected by themselves to bring business resources to bear on the country's social problems on the massive scale that is needed. To achieve this, government must create the market conditions that will introduce business enterprises to apply their operational capabilities to those public tasks they can carry out more efficiently than other institutions.[1]

## "WHAT'S-IN-IT-FOR-ME?" FACTOR

Proposition four is particularly worthy of note. I recently discussed social responsibility with the operations manager of a Massachusetts foundry.

"There's nothing wrong with the concept," he told me. "In my book it ranks with motherhood, brotherhood, and be kind to dumb animals."

I asked him to elaborate and he did so.

"There's not a person I know who wouldn't like to see safe and clean streets, poverty and prejudice eliminated, a pure and healthful environment. But that's as far as it usually goes; when it narrows down to specifics, it's another matter entirely."

He illustrated with a story that explained what he meant. He was being pressured by headquarters management to install pollution control equipment and place more women and blacks in key managerial jobs. During the past two or three years, he admitted, he paid lip service and little more to these demands.

"I'd comply more wholeheartedly," he added, "if I could make these moves profitably, or at least break even on them. Thus far I've found no way to do so. My year-end bonus and salary adjustment are tied directly to the earnings I produce. In a broader context, holding on to my job and moving up in the company depend on the bottom line figure as well. If it could somehow be arranged that profit performance was rated on the bottom line figure *plus* the cost of controlling pollution and hiring minorities to help run the company, it would make going along a good deal easier."

Some companies are attemping to do just that, to build social performance into managerial assessments. And some government planners are working hard on new ways to alter the reward process so as to make social investment more palatable to individual corporations and executives— public incentives for private involvement. I view this as yet another growing trend in the years ahead.

## Market Incentives

If productivity is the leading challenge for business leaders in the seventies and eighties, it will be even more of a challenge for government administrators. It's no secret to anyone that many federal, state, and municipal bureaucracies are overridden with inefficiency and waste. As Dr. Laurence J. Peter wryly states the case: "Incompetence plus incompetence equals incompetence—attempts to relieve incompetence increases the number of incompetents and still there is no improvement in efficiency."[2]

Add competition, however, and you may stir up the pot. A classic example is New York City's sanitation problem. A consultant's study a few years back revealed that it cost the

Sanitation Department approximately $50 a ton to haul refuse away; private contractors do the same job for about $18 a ton.

Government-provided market incentives to business can multiply productivity in any number of problem areas from housing and the environment to education and transportation.

In 1970, the Banneker Elementary School in Gary, Indiana, became the country's first public school to be operated by a private concern. Under a contract with the Gary board of education, Behavioral Research Laboratories of Palo Alto, California, took over the school, reorganized and staffed it, paid rent on the building, and provided all learning materials—for the city's calculated cost of $800 per student. At the end of three years, according to the contract, the firm is supposed to refund the fee paid for any of the 840 black students who have not been brought up to or above national grade level norms in all basic curriculum areas (about 75 percent have been below such norms).[3]

I have heard of no such commitment from a municipally operated public school system anywhere in the country. Clearly market incentives offered by government to the private sector present a potential for achievement that is well worth exploring. Feasible applications cover a wide range of social activities.

We already have seen what low-rate FHA mortgage loans, government rent supplements, and the like can do to spark ghetto redevelopment and provide adequate low-income housing. We know how special tax breaks and financial aid for minority hiring and training programs can induce companies to set up shop in economically depressed areas. And I could cite numerous cases of imaginative reward mechanisms set up to lure doctors and health care facilities to serve the underserved poor.

Similarly, a host of incentives could be—and some are in the process of being—dreamed up to motivate environmental cleanup, provide venture capital to refurbish decaying cities, and create new cities from coast to coast.

Even with optimum cooperation between the public and private sectors, the job won't be easy. Thorny problems relating to life styles, values, and dozens of other issues remain to be tackled and solved. But government and business partnership has solved thornier problems in the past. We have enough successes behind us to provide the direction we need to multiply productivity and extend the social dollar on a variety of fronts.

Mounting evidence proves that the private sector is uniquely well qualified to fulfill many of the social goals facing us more economically and expeditiously than government working alone. Before the end of this decade I can visualize a wholesale expansion of existing incentives along with a spate of new reward strategies introduced to America's socio-economic system. Increasingly, I believe, this will help to change the attitude of many businessmen regarding social involvement. I look forward to the day, in fact, when competition to engage in government–business programs will be every bit as spirited as competition for the consumer dollar is today.

I think that in the years to come we will see more veterans' and other hospitals run by private entrepreneurs. We will witness an unprecedented wave of cash subsidies, special loans, preferred insurance rates, income guarantees, and tax breaks in a host of public service areas.

We will also see organized a rash of public–private corporations on the order of Comsat and Amtrak. They will be formed to explore new technology, engage in new city planning and development, modernize transportation, introduce new efficiencies into U.S. postal service, make the nation's rail system economically feasible and viable, bring order to our chaotic court and law enforcement networks.

Government–business partnership for progress is a natural. Government possesses the planning savvy and political experience. It has the access to the public borrowing and vast financing required for ambitious large-scale programs. Business possesses the managerial know-how and experience, research and implementation capability, technical and marketing skill to get the job done productively and on schedule.

Within both of these resources combined lies the strength of America.

## Social Reporting: What Lies Ahead?

The year was 1951. The company had problems. Business was booming, orders piling up to the rafters. Transactions occurred more rapidly than they could be recorded and reported. Business had never been better. But management felt it was operating in a vacuum and was becoming alarmed. It wasn't getting the information it required quickly enough to make decisions on time. When reports did come through they were often inaccurate. Gauging production, purchasing, manpower requirements, and storage and distribution needs was becoming a hit or miss proposition.

As the situation was reaching crisis proportions, the president called in a management consultant to review and advise. He studied the problem and proposed a sophisticated management information system that would permit month-end closings in two days instead of three weeks, maintain a running inventory analysis, include built-in checks and balances to ensure absolute accuracy of computer-contained data that could be made available at a moment's notice.

The president was relieved. He wasn't quite sure what the consultant meant when he talked about real time, core storage, and random access. But he was an expert, seemed to know his subject well, and could sell. The company approved his proposal to set up a system.

The system took twice as long to install as anticipated, cost twice as much, produced a paycheck for a custodian in the amount of $3,x14c,9L and showed stockout positions on items that had been overproduced. The company's simple problems were over. It was now in a state of chaos.

The point of the story is this. Social reporting today is

about at the point of development that data and management information systems stood at the start of the fifties. Self-appointed experts are sprouting all over the lot with all kinds of theories and proposals. As in the early days of the computer, for each depth thinker the system spawns two dozen surface scratchers who, well-intentioned or not, substitute labels for concepts and seek to promote decision paralysis on the one extreme, nutcake schemes on the other.

But such is the nature of progress. Out of the great rash of EDP experimentation, theorizing, conceptualizing, and trial-and-errorizing of the fifties emerged a solid base of genuine expertise and data-handling capability. Almost every major corporation today can boast an advanced management information system that cuts clerical workloads to a fraction, provides early warning signals when standards and goals fall behind, adds to communications a new dimension of speed, accuracy, and dependability.

From where I stand, social reporting appears to be traveling this identical route. It is well over a decade since serious thinking and dialogue on the subject got under way. Along with the inevitable shallow proposals, ill-advised experiments, and questionable studies, a storehouse of valuable concepts, methods, and techniques—many of them already proven—has been established. Several leading corporations have taken the time and effort to document early measurement and reporting experiments and record what they learned.

We're now ready to move down the field toward the goalposts, to put what we know and learned into practice. The problem now is to sort the fluff from the substance. For this we will need the organizational machinery to get the process working and the personnel to man the equipment.

What I'm talking about is a clearing house for social information where public and private executives could assemble to introduce new concepts, review case experiences, exchange ideas. Such a center—or series of centers—might be set up in some such place as UCLA, Harvard, the University of Illinois, or other educational institution that already has demonstrated pioneering leadership in the field of social restructuring. Staffed by trained professionals, and equipped with a well-stocked social library, the Social Information Center (SIC, if you like labels) well might be formed and funded under the aegis of the Peace Production Board.

In such an environment, consensus on specific actions to take and directions to establish could be hammered out by multidisciplinary task forces set up to promote corporate social responsibility on an industry-by-industry basis.

### CORPORATE RATINGS ON THE WAY

Let's project into the future. It is Monday, August 17, 1983. A meeting is in process at the offices of XYZ Manufacturing Company. Present are two production managers and the vice president of purchasing. Under discussion is the proposed procurement of a "big ticket" piece of machinery.

Five competing companies had been called in to bid on the order. Two suppliers, ABC Corporation and CBA Enterprises, wound up in the running. So close were they in fact on price, quality, and service backup, that the race is neck and neck.

Nonetheless, the decision presents no problem for the purchasing man and his associates. They unanimously select ABC Corporation with a minimum of discussion. Reason: In the Corporate Social Responsibility ratings published by *Newsweek*, *Wall Street Journal*, *Time*, *The New York Times*, and other leading publications, ABC consistently ranked close to the top of its industry while CBA was listed close to the bottom.

Is this far-fetched hypothesizing? I don't think so.

In an early issue of *Business & Society*, the editor posed some interesting questions: "How does General Electric stack up against Westinghouse? Is General Motors more responsive to social change than Ford? Why is Scott Paper the only company in the paper industry to have named a black to its board of directors? [This was in the January

*212*

1972 issue.] Why is an employee retiring from Sears Roebuck in much better financial shape than a retiree from the Great Atlantic & Pacific Tea Company? Which company is more closely attuned to consumer needs—RCA or Whirlpool? Is U.S. Steel the most fiercesome polluter in the steel industry because it's the largest company or because it has been reluctant or unable to make the necessary investments in environmental protection?"

Such questions demand answers, insists the editor, and he asserts that the answers will be forthcoming. I agree. Individual and institutional investors are demanding the answers. So are citizen groups and the public. What's more, pressured increasingly by their constituents, politicians seek answers as well.

So once again we run up against the alternatives: voluntarily or imposed? Undoubtedly both. But imposition is rarely pleasant, and the more voluntary compliance, the less need for laws.

The trend is already well under way. Increasingly, major corporations from manufacturing to service organizations are experimenting with internal social reports. More than ever before, large foundations, public interest auditors, and measurement experts hired to assess corporate social responsibility for institutional groups are probing the actions of business and drawing comparisons between the Texacos and Mobils, the Macys and Gimbels, the Lever Brothers and Proctor and Gambles, the Bristol-Myerses and Lilys.

At the Stanford Business School, a student group which calls itself the Committee for Corporate Responsibility rates organizations on the basis of assigned performance rankings. Conducted on an industry level (canning, for one), the basic analysis consists of a three-dimensional matrix: (1) a breakdown of plants within the industry; (2) a listing of areas of concern for the industry; (3) various means of company-by-company comparison in terms of geography, local legal requirements, potential for positive action, cooperation with efforts to bring about social improvement.

We also are, or should be, moving into a new era of technology assessment, according to David M. Kiefer, senior editor of *Chemical and Engineering News.* "What it gets down to," he notes, "is that the profit motive and the traditional market mechanism that we have long relied upon no longer appear to be sufficient for the task of sorting out what technology should be used—and how. The first-order effects of damming a river, or launching a supersonic transport, or introducing a new detergent additive or pesticide, or building a highway may stand out clearly after the customary cost-benefit analysis. Technology assessment would try to get at what else might happen but be overlooked, whether it be beneficial or harmful."

He goes on to explain that technology assessment would scrutinize the interactions, side effects, by-products, spillovers, and trade-offs among several developing technologies or between a new technology and society at large and the environment. Hence the forecasting of technology would uncover potential problems at the same time it would disclose opportunities that might be overlooked.

"Technology assessment," states Kiefer, "offers us the hope of making technology our servant rather than our master." But, he adds, who is to do it? How and where will it be done?

Perhaps what industry needs is a counter commercial development staff or long-range debunking group within the over-all corporate structure. Such a group would assess business objectives and priorities not merely in the customary terms of short-range profits and sales growth but also in terms of social responsibility and consequences.

Here is yet another exciting challenge for a Peace Production Board to tackle.

In any event, I don't think I'd be far off in predicting that well before the middle of the next decade social assessment and reporting will be commonly practiced. Certainly, all other factors being equal or close to equal, a company's social responsibility rating will be a key determinant where such decisions as purchasing (retail and wholesale), investment, and, most assuredly, employment, are under consideration. The more educated the public becomes, the more important this will be. As exposure expands and pressures increase, the learning rate must inevitably accelerate.

Long-range planning is nothing new to growth-minded captains of industry. What appears certain to accelerate in the next few years from what I have observed, is futures research and planning with a focus on the corporate conscience as well as on earnings. I think great numbers of business leaders will be trying to gauge the effects of company policies and actions on human beings and the environment.

As General Electric Company's Ian H. Wilson observed, we are being confronted by an accelerating incidence of discontinuities in our society and in our business operations. They are created by technology, by changes in our value system, by such trends as affluence and education "going critical" almost to the point of being revolutionary.

What can be done about it?

GE's response, representative of a growing trend, is worth noting. In the company's initial environment study, started in early 1967 and described in part in chapter five, says Wilson, "We reviewed a broad spectrum of changes that might develop in the United States over the next ten years. It was an attempt, through identifying these forces for change, to make sense of change, to see a pattern in the kaleidoscope of events and trends."

GE got off to an early start, but not too early. Clearly, an ample cushion of lead time is required if systematic corporate changes are to develop.

GE's study was necessarily broad and relatively superficial, derived from a wide range of external inputs, interviews, literature, and the like. Forecasts were made, then reevaluated a year later. Getting results into print was important, the study group feels. For one thing, this process produced a whole new set of inputs to be factored into future analyses. One purpose in conducting the study was to help define priorities for future research. It came as no surprise, notes Wilson, that the urban/minority problem was identified as the principal domestic problem of the next decade.

The program focused on the long-term forces at work in the minority environment, rather than on the obvious current issues. One thing made clear was the long-term persistence of the problem, its complexity, and the inadequacy of corporate response to date inside General Electric or elsewhere.

The program's end product was more than reports. As a result of its findings, General Electric established for the first time at the corporate level an Equal Opportunity/Minority Relations component to translate into action the company's long-term commitment. States Wilson: "We in Business Environment worked with this newly established component in what I think can justifiably be termed the first 'systems approach' (by a corporation, at least) to the minority problem."

He adds, translating the very general guidelines of the study into specific programs designed to bring about change, is "a hard, slogging, time-consuming, sometimes frustrating—but exciting—challenge." It took a task force of twenty-seven people a year to take apart the company's manpower system piece by piece, analyze each component to determine how far it impeded or helped attain true equality of opportunity, then put the pieces together again into an integrated system.

Wilson lays special stress on the management's measurement and reward system. "If society is re-writing its 'charter of expectations' of corporations," he says, "if society is going to judge business performance by new criteria, then we must start to measure our own performance by new criteria —and soon! Otherwise all the best laid plans, all the most eloquent and sincere policy statements, will founder on the rock of inadequate performance. Managers are rational human beings—economic men, if you will—who will perform as they know they are to be measured."[4]

216

Here in its essence is one of the important points I am attempting to present.

## The Pipeline Requirement

One day last month I received a telephone call from a former business associate who is now president of a medium-sized distributing company. I'll refer to him as Jim.

Jim knows I have long been active in promoting the principles of socio-economic management and attempting to get social measurement and reporting out of the classroom and into the field. Like thousands of other thoughtful businessmen, Jim is deeply concerned regarding the ills of society, especially those produced by business. In the past we had engaged in long discussions on the subject, and had done some soul-searching together.

Now Jim told me that some time back he and some other executives had organized a small private investment club. The topic of corporate social responsibility had come up at one of their meetings. Most of the members, like Jim, were concerned about the subject. If they could possibly help it, they didn't want to invest their money in socially irresponsible companies. Jim asked me for some help.

"What can I say, Jim? I appreciate your concern. But many people are wrestling with the same question."

Jim told me what he'd like is some names.

I explained that I wasn't in the investment business and couldn't in good conscience make specific recommendations.

"I suspected you'd say that," Jim replied. "All right, then, how about a list of companies to avoid?"

"I'm not qualified for that, either. What I can do is send you some studies and ratings made by a handful of publications and organizations. You'll find them limited and some a bit slanted, but that's the best you can do at this point."

Jim thanked me and said he would settle for that.

217

The story points up a crucial social need. I believe we're on the brink of an unprecedented research explosion in America, and rightly so. At all levels of social decision, managers and administrators are confronted by a glaring intelligence gap. Information pipelines are missing; responsible decision-makers have no place to turn for reliable and comprehensive information.

Information pipelines are missing for the concerned investor, individual, private group, or institution wishing to make investment decisions that are financially advantageous without being socially destructive.

They are missing for the concerned manager who would like to assess the effects of his company's decisions and policies on the consumer and community.

They are lacking for the dedicated institutional administrator who wishes to determine the effectiveness of social programs and innovations in fulfilling human needs.

They are lacking for the responsible government official who wants to monitor corporate and institutional performance within his constituency, apply social pressures where called for, propose legislation where needed to achieve social improvement.

As my executive friend Jim can attest, socio-economic intelligence is hard to come by in a great many areas where it is critically required. Notes *Time* magazine: "They [economists] cannot gauge the severity of the labor shortages that are raising production costs by forcing businessmen to rely on untrained and inefficient workers. The Government collects no figures on job vacancies to match against its thorough reports on the number of workers unemployed. More surprisingly, no one really knows how rapidly wage costs are rising."

The same story is duplicated in a host of other areas from health care and transportation to housing and the environment. "The deficiencies are great enough," *Time* adds, "to raise the question of how the economy is managed at all. The answer is plain enough: imperfectly."

BOOSTER SHOT

There are two schools of thought when it comes to the subject of social research.

An academic friend recently cautioned: "Social change can't be hammered through with a pile driver. It must be undertaken slowly and gradually. We don't have a fraction of the research we'll need to get social reports under way."

That's school number one: research first, action later. I asked my friend if he knew where the line labeled "enough" should be drawn. He had no answer.

School of thought number two is the "let's get started" school. Action has been too long delayed already.

This neither bypasses nor underrates the need for well-planned and generously funded research plus the wholesale expansion of information pipelines to investors, administrators, corporate executives, community leaders, and government officials. School of thought number two heartily endorses all moves in this direction.

My argument is not for research or action, it's for research *and* action. One clearly abets the other. We already possess an impressive backlog of experience and expertise. A major national drive for corporate social reports in all important industries is long overdue.

I concede that no thoughtful student of business and society could pretend that complex problems do not exist. But the recommendations I have proposed in this book would go a long way toward simplifying concepts and procedures. They will not yield perfect measures and reports, but I think they would produce reports that will serve as rough road maps at first and in a relatively short time will be about as accurate as most financial reports are today. A long way from the ultimate, but practical and useful. Research plus action follow-up would plug many of the intelligence gaps mentioned in this and other chapters. It would encourage measurement and reporting patterns to evolve and standardize more rapidly, efficiently, and on a more orderly basis. It would help us to minimize errors and misjudgments, reduce the incidence and cost of adjustments and corrections later on.

In what specific areas should we concentrate research expansion efforts?

Devising alternative methods of measurement, for one. A Social Information Center might set about collecting existing documentation on the subject, of which there is a wealth. It could then organize meetings and seminars that would be attended by executives, accountants, sociologists, and scholars with experience and savvy in this area. What would inevitably emerge would be the best and most successful models developed to date. The same thing could be done with social reports, using the Socio-Economic Operating Statement or some similar format as a launching pad model, with innovations and refinements as the learning process solidifies.

There are numerous procedures in industry to report and evaluate, set up information systems, structure corporate manpower units, and perform various management functions. Research might well disclose that the pattern of measurement and reporting applicable to the oil industry is not applicable to the steel industry. Thus research studies might be required on the industry as well as general corporate or national levels. Another likely area of exploration might be into potentials of corporate gain through social contributions. This would tie in naturally with studies on incentives, strategies to motivate corporate social responsibility where such motivation might be presently lacking.

As we approach the second half of this decade, we find a growing accumulation of corporate case histories that describe specific measurement techniques, reporting formats, areas of responsibility covered, roadblocks and resistance encountered. We must probe deeper into existing inequities, competitive advantages under varying circumstances, errors made in attempting to set up social responsibility programs.

I have come across innumerable talks, seminar reports, conference proceedings, articles, and books dealing with these and other aspects. But simply pulling together the materials for this book has been a rather arduous procedure. The whole body of information on this crucially important subject of corporate social responsibility has been established and shelved on a generally scattershot basis. A well-organized and narrowly focused research/cataloging effort would help centralize all knowledge on the subject, differentiate between models that work and models that flop, assist the social building and refinement process on an ongoing basis as was done in the past with various economic models which now serve society well.

## HUMAN RESOURCE ACCOUNTING

A good start in a related direction already has been made by the University of Michigan Graduate School of Business Administration's Human Resource Association. HRA memberships are available to representatives of business, government, universities, nonprofit and other organizations.

HRA's principal goal is to "provide members with quantitative cost/benefit information about human resources to improve the allocation, utilization, and return on total organizational resources (physical and human)." To achieve this purpose, members "develop new methods to identify and record qualitative cost/benefit information about human resources; promote the application and use of these new methods; communicate and disseminate information about these new methods."

HRA schedules an annual conference to "report and review the prior year's activities; plan measurement, decision area, and informational exchange activities for the following year; make committee and study group appointments."

Participating in these activities are representatives of major U.S. corporations, accounting firms, and nonprofit organizations. Study groups analyze specific case histories and tackle such problems as employee dissatisfaction and its causes; the care and nursing of human resources; employee hiring, training, and recruitment.

Expanded to encompass social measurement and reporting and a broader range of social research areas, the organizational concept and structure has a good deal to offer.

## The Option for Orderly Change

At a White House Conference on the Industrial World Ahead in Washington, D.C., in 1972, Dr. Willis W. Harman, director of Stanford Research Institute's Educational Policy Research Center, said, "Several clues indicate that the industrialized world may be experiencing the beginning phase of a socio-cultural revolution as profound and pervasive in its effects on all segments of the society as the Industrial Revolution, the Reformation, or the Fall of Rome."

He cites the following "lead indicators of revolutionary change":

- decreased sense of community
- increased sense of alienation and purposelessness
- increased occurrence of violent crime
- increased frequency of personal disorders and mental illness
- increased frequency and severity of social disruptions
- increased use of police to control behavior
- increase in amount of noninstitutionalized religious activities

"To anyone who has read the newspapers over the last decade," notes Dr. Harman, "the list alone makes the point."[5]

Revolution, orderly social change? The choice is up to all of us. I see the rising pressures on corporations both from inside and outside of business as symptomatic of the danger Dr. Harman refers to. Anything short of drastic improvement will serve only to heighten frustrations and produce heat in place of reason. Rising expectations can no longer exist in harmony with tight-lipped status quo intractability.

Sooner or later they must clash.

It is my sincere belief that well-reasoned socio-economic management, social measurement, and reporting as proposed in this book would go a long way toward helping to avoid such conflict.

# NOTES

## CHAPTER 1

1. *New York Times,* 11 March 1973, p. 17.
2. *Corporate Responsibility and Religious Institutions,* (New York: Corporate Information Center, National Council of Churches, October 1971), p. 22.
3. Eleanore Carruth, "The 'Legal Explosion' Has Left Business Shell-Shocked," *Fortune,* April 1973, p. 67.
4. *Business Leadership in Social Change,* (New York: The Conference Board, 1971), pp. 3-4.

## CHAPTER 2

1. John Diebold, "The Social Responsibility of Business" (Paper presented at Ministry of Economics and Finance Meeting, Paris, France, June 21, 1972).
2. Alvin Toffler, *Future Shock,* (New York: Random House, 1970) p. 400.
3. Arjay Miller, "National Goals and Priorities" (Talk given at Conference Board Public Affairs Conference, New York City, 14 April 1971).

## CHAPTER 4

1. G. Robert Truex, "Term 'Social Audit' Should Be Dropped," *The American Banker,* 16 May 1973.
2. Gilbert Burck, "The Hazards of Corporate Responsibility," *Fortune,* June 1973, p. 216.
3. Daniel Yankelovich, "The New Odds" (Paper presented at the Eleventh Annual Marketing Strategy Conference of the Sales Executive Club of New York, New York, 15 October 1971).
4. Alice Marlin, *Social Measurement* (New York: American Institute of Certified Public Accountants, 1972), p. 46.
5. *New York Times,* 2 April 1973, p. 55.

225

## CHAPTER 5

1. Raymond A. Bauer and Dan H. Fenn, Jr., "What *Is* a Corporate Social Audit?", *Harvard Business Review*, January-February 1973.
2. John J. Corson, "A Corporate Social Audit?", *The Center Magazine*, January/February 1972, p. 62.

## CHAPTER 7

1. U.S., Congress, Senate, Consumer Subcommittee, Committee on Commerce, *Initiatives in Corporate Responsibility*, prepared by Hon. Frank E. Moss, Chairman, 92nd Cong., 2d sess., 2 October 1972, p. 316.
2. U.S., Office of Management and Budget, *Social Indicators*, 1973.
3. Alice Marlin, *Social Measurement* (New York: American Institute of Certified Public Accountants, 1972), pp. 98-101.

## CHAPTER 8

1. "How To Put Corporate Responsibility Into Practice," *Business and Society Review*, Summer 1973, p. 11.
2. G. Robert Truex, "Term 'Social Audit' Should Be Dropped," *The American Banker*, 16 May 1973.
3. John L. Paluszek, *Organizing for Corporate Social Responsibility*, Special Study 51 (New York: The President's Association, Inc., Winter 1972-73), p. 34.
4. Ralph Nader and Mark Green, eds., *Corporate Power in America* (New York: Grossman, 1973), pp. 154-58.
5. Meinolf Dierkes and Robert Coppock, "Corporate Responsibility Does Not Depend on Public Pressure," *Business and Society Review*, Summer 1973, p. 87.

## CHAPTER 9

1. George A. Steiner, "The Business Social Audit" (Paper presented at Social Audit Conference, University of California, Los Angeles, May 23-25, 1972), Proceedings of Conference, p. 47.

## CHAPTER 10

1. Steven M. Director and Samuel I. Doctors, "Do Business School Students Really Care About Social Responsibility?" *Business and Society Review/Innovation*, Spring 1973, p. 91.

2. Ralph Nader and Mark Green, eds., *Corporate Power in America*, p. 162.

3. Grace J. Finley, *Policies on Leaves For Political and Social Action*, Report No. 554, (New York: The Conference Board), p. 1.


CHAPTER 11


1. Committee for Economic Development, *Social Responsibilities of Business Corporations*, June 1971, p. 51.

2. Dr. Laurence J. Peter and Raymond Hull, *The Peter Principle: Why Things Go Wrong* (New York: William Morrow, 1969), p. 107.

3. Committee for Economic Development, *Social Responsibilities of Business Corporations*, June 1971, p. 54.

4. Ian H. Wilson, "Futures Planning: A New Dimension of the Corporate Planner" (Address given at the International Conference on Corporate Planning, Montreal, December 8, 1971).

5. Willis W. Harman, "Key Choice of the Next Two Decades" (Speech given at White House Conference on the Industrial World Ahead, Washington, D.C., February 7-9, 1972).

# INDEX

# Index

## ABOUT THE AUTHOR

**David F. Linowes** developed the concept of Socio-Economic Management, which is the application of successful business management principles, modified by social science techniques, to our governmental and social institutions. These principles have attained widespread recognition among government officials, industrialists, and educators and are embodied in his book *Strategies for Survival,* the 1973 Membership Book selection of the American Management Association.

As a consultant to the U.S. Department of State, he headed missions to Turkey, India, and Greece. In 1968, he undertook for the United Nations a mission involving Pakistan, Iran, and Turkey. Mr. Linowes also served as an adviser to the Department of Health, Education and Welfare during John W. Gardner's tenure.

Mr. Linowes is a partner in the worldwide auditing and consulting firm of Laventhol Krekstein Horwath & Horwath and was the Distinguished Arthur Young Visiting Professor for 1973–1974 at the University of Illinois. He is a member of the boards of directors of Chris Craft Industries, Inc., The Horn & Hardart Company, Inc., Piper Aircraft Corporation, and Saturday Review/World Magazine, Inc. Mr. Linowes recently served as chairman of the Trial Board of the American Institute of Certified Public Accountants and is a former adjunct professor of management, New York University. From 1970 through 1973 he was chairman and chief executive officer of Mickleberry Corporation.

In addition to *Strategies for Survival,* his earlier works include *Managing Growth Through Acquisition,* which was a selection of The Presidents Association, and many articles for such leading publications as *The New York Times, Nation's Business,* and *The Journal of Accountancy.*